Repair Instructions

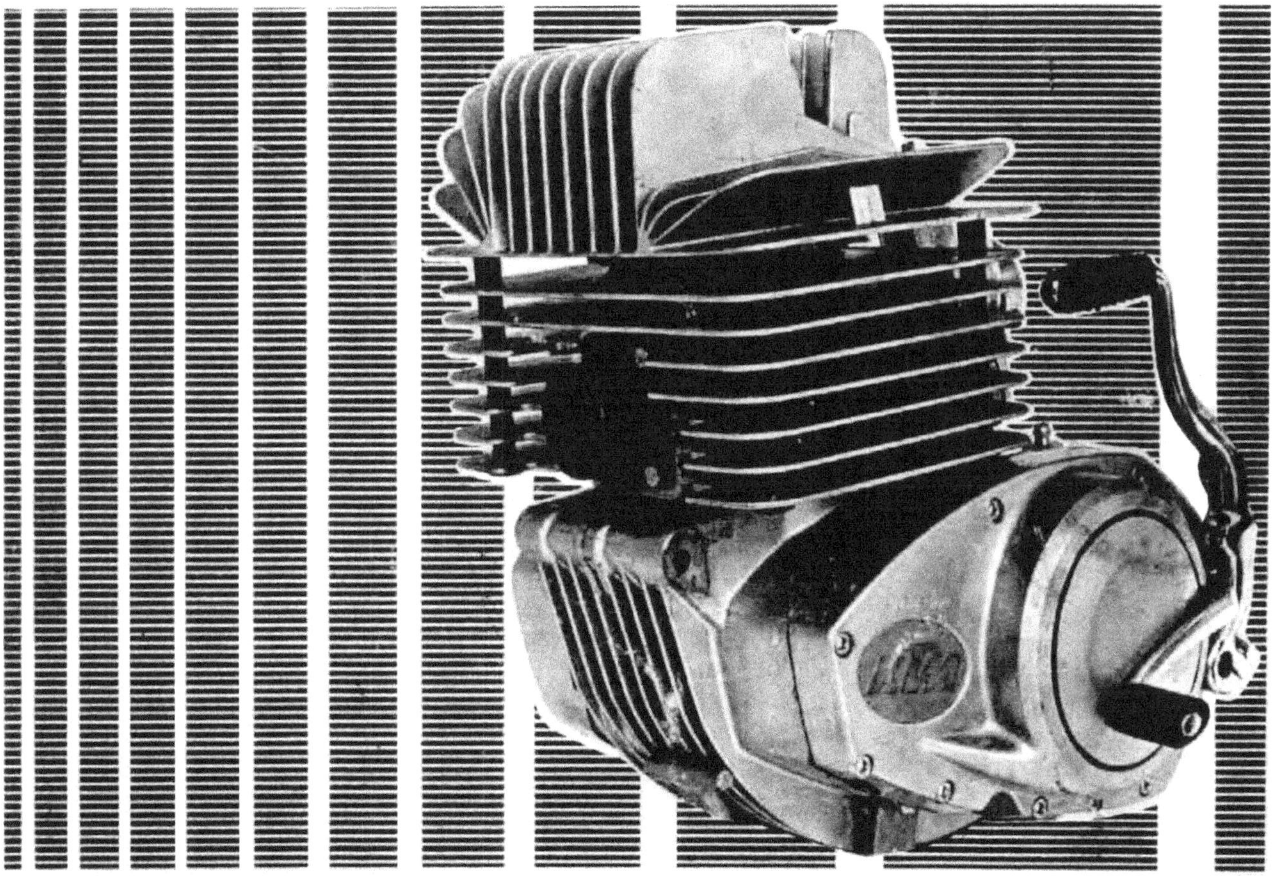

**Engine 125
175
250
400 cc**

PREFACE

TRADEMARKS & COPYRIGHT

Penton® and KTM® are the registered trademarks of Penton, Inc. and Pierer Mobility AG. This publication is not sponsored by or endorsed by the trademark owners. We recognize that some words, model names and designations, for example, mentioned herein are the property of the trademark holder. We use them for identification purposes only. This is not an official publication however; it may include non-copyright works of the trademark holder.

INTRODUCTION

Welcome to the world of digital publishing ~ the book you now hold in your hand was printed using the latest state of the art digital technology. The advent of print-on-demand has forever changed the publishing process, never has information been so accessible and it is our hope that this book serves your informational needs for years to come. If this is your first exposure to digital publishing, we hope that you are pleased with the results. Many more titles of interest to the classic automobile and motorcycle enthusiast, collector and restorer are available via our website at www.VelocePress.com. We hope that you find this title as interesting as we do.

NOTE FROM THE PUBLISHER

The information presented is true and complete to the best of our knowledge. All recommendations are made without any guarantees on the part of the author or the publisher, who also disclaim all liability incurred with the use of this information.

INFORMATION ON THE USE OF THIS PUBLICATION

This manual is an invaluable resource for those interested in performing their own maintenance. However, in today's information age we are constantly subject to changes in common practice, new technology, availability of improved materials and increased awareness of chemical toxicity. As such, it is advised that the user consult with an experienced professional prior to undertaking any procedure described herein. While every care has been taken to ensure correctness of information, it is obviously not possible to guarantee complete freedom from errors or omissions or to accept liability arising from such errors or omissions. Therefore, any individual that uses the information contained within, or elects to perform or participate in do-it-yourself repairs or modifications acknowledges that there is a risk factor involved and that the publisher or its associates cannot be held responsible for personal injury or property damage resulting from the use of the information or the outcome of such procedures.

WARNING!

One final word of advice, this publication is intended to be used as a reference guide, and when in doubt the reader should consult with a qualified technician.

FORWORD

This repair manual concerns a high powered engine. It is natural for such engines to be developed and therefore they are subject to alterations. For this reason it is possible for this repair manual to be out of date in respect of certain particulars. However by means of numbered customers' after - sales bulletins we endeavour to inform you of alterations of settings and design so long as these are of any importance. As a consequence we are not obliged to amend this repair manual.

KTM-Motor-Fahrzeugbau KG.

INDEX

TYPES OF ENGINES	3
TECHNICAL DATA	4 – 5
Repair tools and assembly devices	6 – 7
Tolerances, Tightening Torque	8
REMOVAL AND REFITTING OF ENGINE	9
ENGINE DISASSEMBLY	9 – 16
WORK ON INDIVIDUAL PARTS	16 – 25
Crank cases: Transmission bearing replacement	
Crankshaft bearing – outer race	16 – 17
Crankshaft: Bearing renewal, Measuring of axial play	18 – 19
Kickstart-installation	19 – 20
Transmission – Drive shaft	21
Output shaft	22
Gear shift	23
Clutch	24
PISTON – PISTON RINGS	25
Piston	25
Piston Rings	25
Gap	25
Cylinder	25
ENGINE ASSEMBLY	26 – 33
Fitting gear transmission	26
Gear change assembly	26
Crankshaft	27
Primary drive clutch	28 – 29
Piston and cylinder	30 – 32
Ignition system	32 – 33
OIL CHECK – OIL CHANGE	34
WIRING SCHEME	34 – 35
CARBURETTOR	36 – 38
AIR FILTER	39
LUBRICATION AND MAINTENANCE PROGRAMME	40
TROUBLE SHOOTING	41
TECHNICAL DRAWINGS	42

PRINTED April 1979

WITHOUT ANY GUARANTEE FOR DESIGNING AND EXECUTION-CHANGES!

Types of Engines

Type 51 – 125 cc
Alternatively 5 or 6 speed transmission

Type 52 – 175 cc
Alternatively 5 or 6 speed transmission

Type 54 – 250 cc
Alternatively 5 or 6 speed transmission

Type 55 – 350/400 cc
Alternatively 5 or 6 speed transmission

TECHNICAL DATA

	125 cc	175 cc	250 cc	400 cc
Design	air-cooled single cylinder – two stroke – engine			
Piston displacement (actual)	124 cc	172 cc	246 cc	359 cc
Bore/Stroke	54/54	63,5/54	71/62	82/68
Performance max.	19,1 kW (26 DIN HP)	20 kW (27 DIN HP)	28 kW (38 DIN HP)	31 kW (42 DIN HP)
RPM at max. h. p.	9700 rpm	8400 rpm	7400 rpm	6700 rpm
Fuel	SUPER Fuel ROZ 98 mixed with two-stroke-oil			
Oil to gasoline mix ratio	VALVOLINE 2 cycle competition oil SAE 40 1:40	CASTROL Super two stroke oil 1:25		BEL-RAY MC-1 Two cycle racing lubricant 1:50
Crankshaft bearings	2 shoulder bearings – 1 Ball bearing			
Connecting rod bearing	needle bearing			
Piston pin bushing	needle bearing			
Piston	light metal – forged			
Piston Rings	1 rectangular ring	1 L-section and 1 rectangular ring		
Measurement „X" Deck height	0,4 – 0,5 mm	0,85 – 0,9 mm	1,1 – 1,15 mm	1,15 – 1,2 mm
Ignition timing B. T. D. C.	0,9 – 0,95 mm	1,9 – 2 mm	2,0 – 2,1 mm	2,25 – 2,3 mm
Sparking plug heat-range	see table 1			
Plug gap	spark plug gap 0.6 mm			
Primary drive	straight-cut gears			
Primary ratio	20:73	20:73	25:69	25:69
Clutch	multiple disc clutch in oil-bath			
Transmission	6-speed (GS) and 5-speed (MC)			
Gear ratios	see table 2			
Gear lubrication	1,6 litres engine-oil HD 20-30 or ATF oil (Autom. Trans. Fluid)			
Ignition system	Motoplat-C. D. I.-ignition system			
Generator output	not used for 125 MC	6 V / 35 / 5 / 21 Watt		
Generator connections		yellow 35 W – white 5 W (inductive) – green 21 W		
Carburettor	BING piston-slide carburettor			
Carburettor setting	see table 3			
Air filter	wet-type air filter insert with foam material			

In order to obtain the correct adjustment after remounting of the cylinder, the measurement „X" has to be strictly adhered to (insertion of differently thick cylinder gaskets). During measurement, the cylinder has to be tightened down and the piston has to be adjusted to the upper dead center.

TABLE 1 — Sparking plug heat range - comparsion table

Enduro	125	175	250	400	MC	125	175	250	400
Champion					Champion	L3G	L3G	L3G	L3G
Bosch	W 340 S 1 S	W 340 S 1 S	W 310 S 1 S	W 310 S 1 S	Bosch	W 340– W 370 S 1 S	W 340 S 1 S	W 340 S 1 S	W 340 S 1 S

Check with your dealer as to best recommandation

TABLE 2 — Gear ratios and top speeds

Primary ratio	Gear ratio	Original secondary gearing ratio	Top speed km/h (RPM at max. h.p.)	Available drive sprockets	Available rear wheel sprockets
125 ccm 20:73	1st gear 14:36	125 GS 13:52	120	12 Z for chain	48 Z for chain
175 ccm	2nd gear 18:32	125 MC 12:57	97	13 Z $1/4 \times 5/8$"	52 Z $1/4 \times 5/8$"
	3rd gear 21:28	175 GS 13:52	104	14 Z	57 Z
	4th gear 24:25	175 MC 13:52	104		
250 ccm 25:69	5th gear 26:23	250 GS 13:52	116	11 Z	48 Z for chain
400 ccm	6th gear 28:21	250 MC 13:57	105	12 Z for chain	52 Z $3/8 \times 5/8$"
	*6th gear 29:21	400 GS 14:52	113	13 Z $3/8 \times 5/8$"	57 Z
		400 MC 13:52	105	14 Z	
	*125 GS, 175 GS			15 Z	

TABLE 3 — Carburettor basic setup

	125 GS	125 MC	175 GS/MC	250 GS	250 MC	400 GS/MC
Type of carburettor	54/34/1040	54/34/1040	54/36/1220	54/36/1220	54/38/107	54/38/107
Main jet	180	185	190	185	185	190
Needle jet	278	280	280	282	282	282
Idling jet	45	45	45	45	45	45
Needle position	2	2	2	2	2	2
Pilot air screw open	¾–1 turn	1 turn	1 turn	1 turn	1 turn	1-1½ turn
Throttle valve	230	220	230	230	220	230

SPECIAL TOOLS FOR KTM ENGINES

Description	No.	125	175	250/400
1. Clamping frame	1	51.12.001.000	51.12.001.000	51.12.001.000
2. Internal washer extractor	1	51.12.002.000	51.12.002.000	52.12.002.000
3. Clutch holder	1	51.12.003.000	51.12.003.000	52.12.003.000
5. Centring pins	3	51.12.005.000	51.12.005.000	51.12.005.000
6. Special screwdriver	1	51.12.006.000	51.12.006.000	51.12.006.000
7. Special hexagon screwdriver	1	51.12.007.000	51.12.007.000	51.12.007.000
8. Retracting mechanism	1	51.12.008.000	51.12.008.000	54.12.008.000
9. Magneto extractor	1	*GS 52.12.009.000 **MC 51.12.009.000	52.12.009.000	52.12.009.000
10. Pointed pliers, reversed	1	51.12.010.000	51.12.010.000	51.12.010.000
11. Special retaining ring pliers, reversed	1	51.12.011.000	51.12.011.000	51.12.011.000
12. Holding spanner for chain wheel and flywheel	1	51.12.012.000	51.12.012.000	51.12.012.000
13. Adjustment gauge for ignition point	1	51.12.013.000	51.12.013.000	51.12.013.000
14. Graduated disc	1	51.12.014.000	51.12.014.000	51.12.014.000
15. Standby gudgeon pin	1	51.12.015.000	51.12.015.000	
16. Protection grommet for flywheel extraction	1	51.12.016.000	51.12.016.000	51.12.016.000
17. Bearing extractor	1	51.12.017.000	51.12.017.000	52.12.017.000
18. Key for kickstarter stop screw	1	51.12.018.000	51.12.018.000	52.12.018.000

* M 26x1.5
** M 27x1

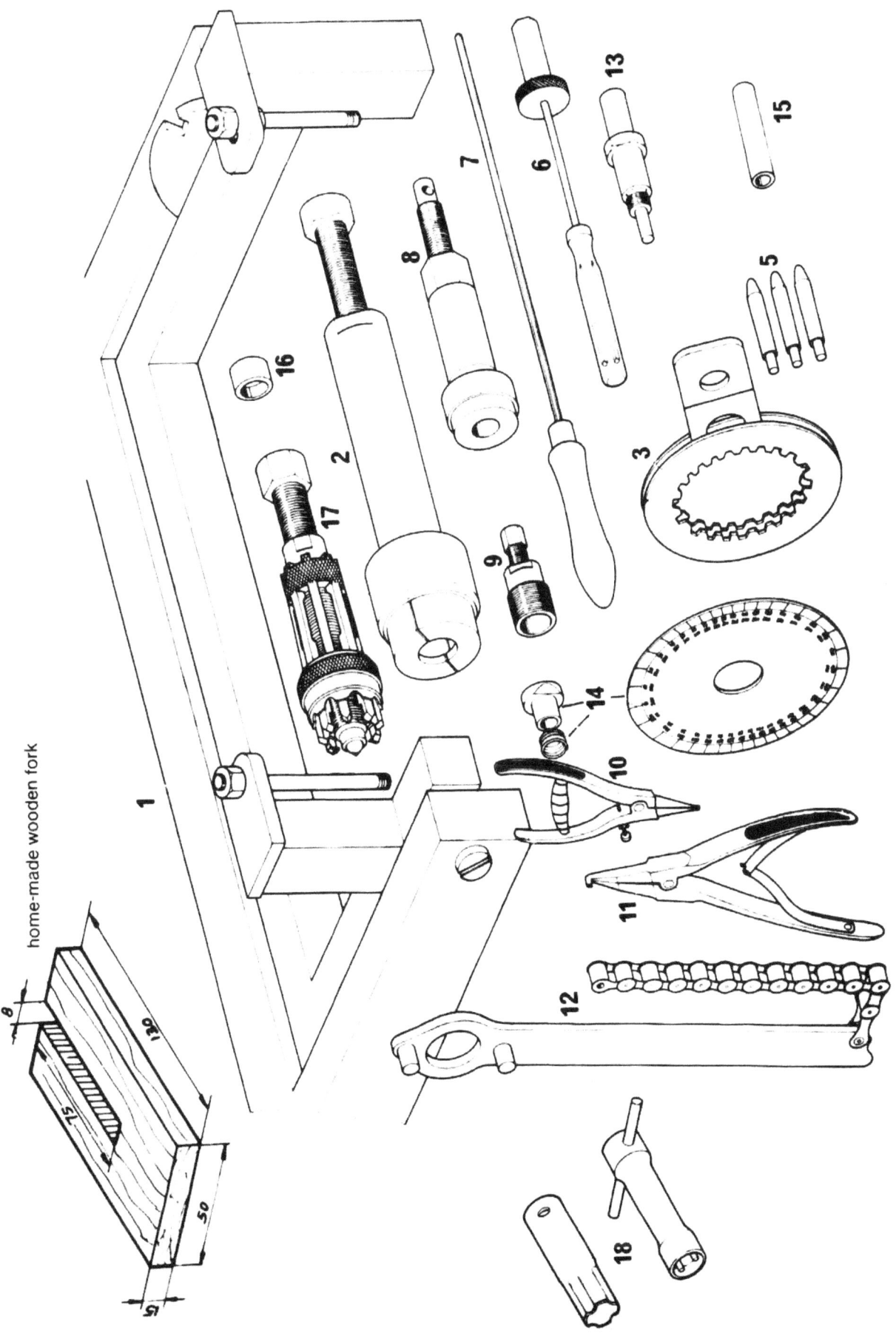

TOLERANCES AND FITTING CLEARANCES	Piston fitting clearance: 125 cc	0,040 – 0,050 mm
	175 cc	0,060 – 0,070 mm
	250 cc	0,060 – 0,080 mm
	400 cc	0,080 – 0,090 mm
	Crankshaft pin oscillation	max. 0,05 mm
	Crankshaft axial clearance	max. 0,06 mm
	Piston ring gap	0,15 – 0,2 mm
	Connecting rod bearing radial	max. 0,06 mm
	Transmission ball bearings – radial clearance	max. 0,05 mm
	End Float of Transmission Shaft	max. 0,1 mm
	Clutch spring lengths	1,5 Ø – 40,5 mm 1,7 Ø – 37 mm
GASKET THICKNESSES (not pressure-fitted)	Engine case	0,3 mm
	Clutch cover	0,3 mm
	Ignition cover	0,3 mm
	Cylinder head gasket	1 mm (400 cc – 1,5 mm)
	Cylinder base gasket	as required
	Available base gaskets	0,2/0,3/0,5/0,75/1 mm
	Crankshaft sealing flange (RH)	0,3 mm
TIGHTENING TORQUE	Cylinder head screw	M 8	125 – 175 29,4 Nm (3 kpm) 250 – 400 34,3 – 39,2 Nm (3,5 – 4 kpm)
	Cylinder nuts and head bolts	M 8	125 – 175 29,4 Nm (3 kpm) 250 – 400 39,2 Nm (4 kpm)
	Magneto flywheel nut (LH thread)	M 12 x 1	54 – 58,9 Nm (5,5 – 6 kpm)
	Countershaft sprocket	M 20 x 1,5	49 Nm (5 kpm)
	Nut for primary sprocket	M 18 x 1,5	54 – 58,9 Nm (5,5 – 6 kpm)
	Nut for inner cluch hub	M 22 x 1,5	68,7 Nm (7 kpm)
	Threaded bushing for kickstarter shaft	M 24 x 1,5	39,2 Nm (4 kpm)
	Engine case and cover screws	M 6	7,8 Nm (0,8 kpm)
	Motor fastening screw	M 12	83,4 Nm (8,5 kpm)
	Motor fastening screw	M 10	49 Nm (5 kpm)
	Swingarm pivot	M 14	137,3 Nm (14 kpm)

Removal and refitting of the engine

Clean the vehicle

Unscrew the ignition housing cover, remove chain, unhook coupling cable to the engine, remove tank, unscrew suction sleeve and cables to the carburettor; disconnect the electrical leads on the terminal strip and ignition coil, remove transmission breather tube. Dismantle exhaust equipment. Unscrew rear engine fixing screw M 12, remove spacer for this purpose, unscrew (if necessary) swivel arm pins, unscrew lower and front engine fixing screws and lift engine out of the frame towards the right.

In this manner the engine is refitted in reverse order.

NOTE

Before tightening the rear engine fixing screws M 12 the swing arm bolt clamping screws must be unscrewed without fail. After tightening the engine fixing screw is tapped with moderate force on the shim with the plastic hammer and only then can the swing arm bolt clamping screws be tightened. If this is not done, the frame in this area can distort and crack at the bolt eyes.

1 Engine fixing screw
2 Swingarm bolt clamping screw
3 Clamp

Engine dismantling

Before being dismantled, the engine must be thoroughly cleaned.

Clamping of the engine

Fix the engine clamping frame in the vice and hold the engine in position with 2 nuts M 10.
Remove kickstarter and foot shift pedal.

Gear oil draining

Unscrew plug 1 and let the oil drain away; replace the drain plug and tighten same.

Cylinder head and Cylinder

Remove the cylinder head after loosening the spacer bolt nuts and screws. Remove the cylinder together with head gasket. Take care that the pistons and piston rings are not damaged. Remove cylinder base gaskets: Uncover crank case, place pistons on wooden assembly frame and remove both gudgeon pin safety stops. Press gudgeon pins out of the pistons without use of force. If necessary, using a gudgeon pin extraction tool. Remove piston and remove gudgeon pin needle bearing from the connecting rod bearing.

Clutch

Turn the engine in the assembly jig so that clutch side will be upwards. Loosen clutch cover screws and remove clutch cover with gasket. (O Ring and spacers on kickstarter shaft in the case of types 54 and 55)

Removal of clutch discs:

Before unscrewing the spring nuts it is recommended that the number of exposed threads be counted, so that after re-assembly the same clutch pressure (spring tension) is obtainable. Withdraw the split pins from the spring bolts and screw out the spring nuts with the special screw driver, where the screwdriver is held fast and the socket used to screw out the nuts.

NOTE

If a spring nut cannot be loosened with the special screwdriver, if for example, the slot of the spring bolt is badly worn, then the following procedure is to be used:

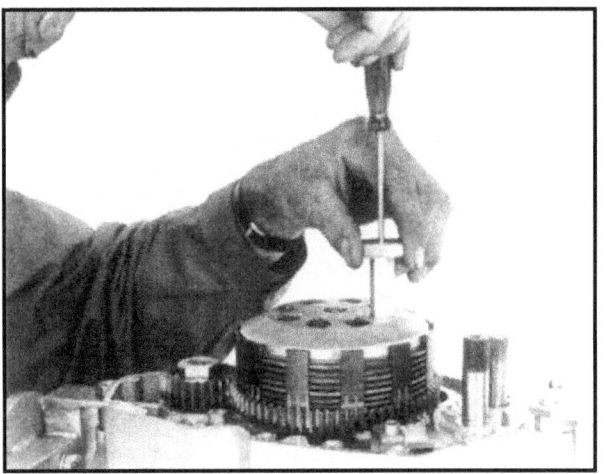

To screw home again as many spring nuts as necessary, so as to make possible satisfactory disengagement of the clutch. Loosen the screwed joints M 8 situated on the right side near the shift lever: Introduce the special hexagon screw driver through the hole which is now free till it meets the opposite casing wall. About 10 mm beyond the right casing wall there is a hole of 6 mm diameter into which the screwdriver is now introduced.

Turn the clutch cage slowly until the special screwdriver reaches the hole found on the back wall of the clutch cage.

Completely disengage the clutch by means of the disengaging lever. Turn pressure cap until the screwdriver touches the head of the damaged spring bolt. Introduce the screwdriver into the hexagonal recess of the bolt head and hold it tight, engage and loosen spring nuts.

The nuts are to be loosened in crosswise order so that the clutch does not jam. Remove the pressure cap and take out the discs, re-screw the spring nuts onto the spring bolts (this makes re-assembly easier). Turn engine slowly in the jig until the clutch side is underneath, so that the two part clutch pressure rod, together with ball in between, falls out from the clutch drive shaft.

(125/175 cc engine)

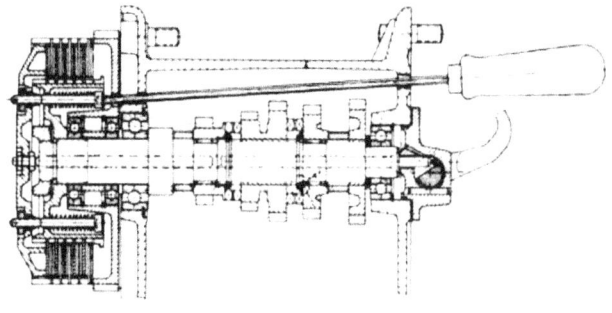

Primary drive

Free locking plates on the crankshaft and clutch drive shaft. Push clutch holder over clutch centre. Make sure that the hole in the handle of the clutch holder is pushed over the kickstarter shaft. Loosen both locking nuts and remove with the locking plates.

Remove primary sprocket, and take out cotter and distance piece.

Pull clutch centre and clutch holder from the drive shaft. Remove clutch cage with check plate.

NOTE

The teeth surfaces of the primary drive are ground and therefore the parts concerned must not be haphazardly interchanged but renewed in pairs only.

Sleeve for controller drum

Remove hexagon recess bolts and pull the sleeve out of the casing.

Ignition System

Loosen flywheel locking screw (left hand thread). The retaining spanner is used for this purpose. In connection with this, it is to be noted that the flywheel is in such a position that when using the retaining spanner the transmitter in the stator is not damaged. Place protection cap on the thread of the crankshaft and apply the flywheel extractor. Take the flywheel off with care and remove cotter from the crankshaft. Remove retaining plate and take away the stator after loosening the three cylinder screws.
Unscrew mounting plate.

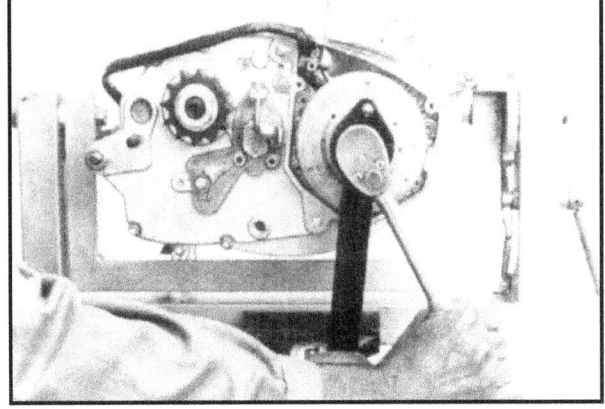

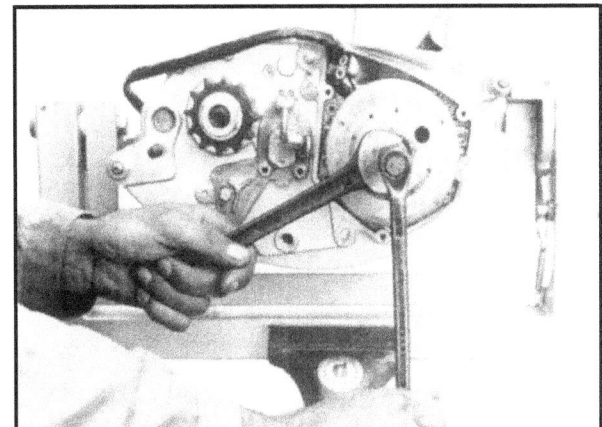

Internal ignition

On engines type 51 with internal ignition first remove retaining plate and then after loosening the 3 screws take off stator. With a wrench (wrench width 32 mm) hold flywheel on its outside hexagon and loosen flywheel locking screw (left hand thread).
Place protection cap on the thread of the crankshaft and apply the flywheel extractor *.
Take the flywheel off with care and remove cotter from the crankshaft.
* M 27x1

(1) Transmitter for ignition
(2) Retaining plate

Chain sprocket

Bend back the chain sprocket nut locking plate. Place the retaining spanner on the chain wheel as shown in the illustration and loosen the nuts; take the chain wheel, distance spacer and O ring from the drive shaft.

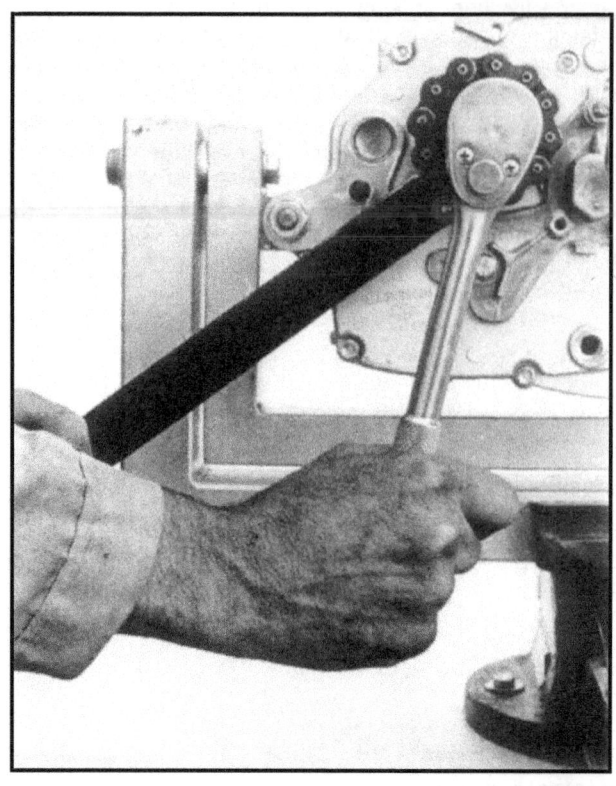

Bearing Cover

Remove bearing cover of the clutch withdrawal device after removal of the locking screws and nuts together with gasket.

Separation of engine casing half sections

Remove all casing screws. Loosen clamping of engine on the jig. Raise right casing half with suitable tools arranged on the cast-on mounts of the casing or separate from the right half by light taps with a plastic hammer on the driven shaft. Separation with a screwdriver being used as a wedge or similar type of separation is to be avoided if at all possible, as sealing surfaces can be slightly damaged.

Take away casing halves and remove gasket.

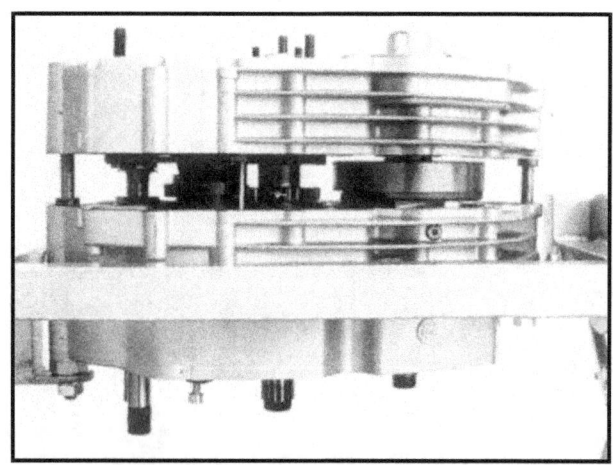

Gear change — Transmission

Take out the gear-shift-lever shaft with the throw out mechanism. Next, remove the controller drum. The gear unit together with the shift fork is taken out of the casing. The gear wheel which remains in the casing is taken out with both thrust washers and the needle bearing and fitted on the driven shaft.

Crankshaft

Take left half of casing off clamping jig. Hold crankshaft by the right crankpin and lift, so that neither crankshaft nor casing touch anywhere. Separate crankshaft from casing by tapping on the casing with a plastic hammer or, when the crankshaft is firmly embedded in the grooved bearing (thrust bearing), press crankshaft out of the half-casing by means of the bearing extractor (I11. 17 of Special Tools).

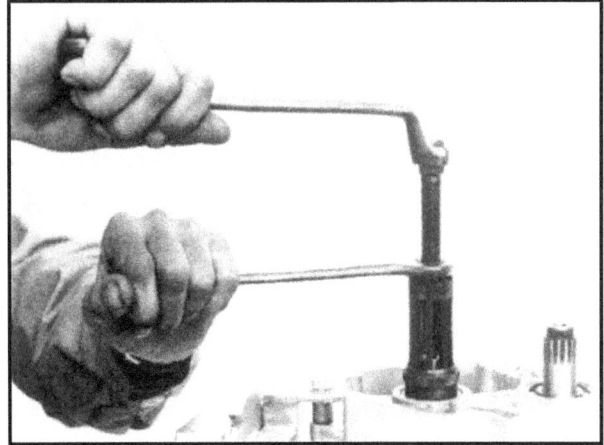

Kickstarter

The kickstarter mechanism, if possible, should only be dismantled if repair of this is necessary.
For disassembly, position casing again on jig and remove the kickstarter top screw on the lower rear part of the engine so that the kickstarter spring is not under tension. In this connection it is to be noted that the kickstarter lever must be pressed down, as otherwise the spring will be suddenly released.

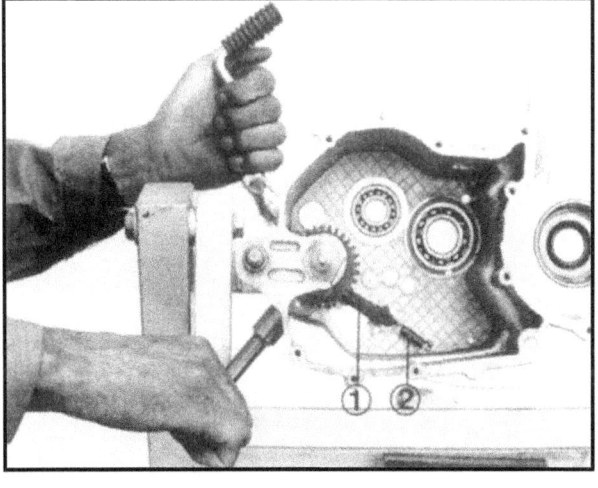

Unlock box screws and screw them out. Take out the kickstarter shaft from above.

Take out of the casing the spring with spring support, kickstarter wheel and kickstarter ratchet wheel. Remove catch after unhooking the tension spring. Clean all parts and check for any wear. If necessary, replace with new parts.

In the case of complete engine overhaul, it is recommended that all gaskets are renewed.

Use only KTM original spare parts.

Work on individual parts

ENGINE CRANK CASE:

Remarks: Before beginning the work you should read once through the following section. Then the sequence of assembly is decided upon so that the bearings can be inserted after preheating the crankcase halves once only.

To press out or, if necessary, also to tap out the bearings, the housing half sections are to be placed on a sufficiently large level surface so that the housing is supported on its complete sealing surface and thus cannot be damaged. Preferably a wooden surface should be used for support.

In the case of changing the crankshaft-collar bearing in particular it is to be noted that outer rings, ball cages and inner rings are not to be mixed up, but they should remain together in groups.

Left crankcase half

Heat the crankcase half by means of a heating plate to 100–150° C and tap the bearings off the driveshaft and output shaft by light tapping inwards with a plastic hammer.

With the half-casing still warm the grooved bearing, the sealing ring holder and the outer ring of the main bearing are pressed in from the outside by means of a drift of approximately the outer diameter of the grooved ball bearing. Take the retaining ring out of the holder and put in a new one in such a way that the packing washer is ejected from the retaining holder and hence towards the crankcase. The lubrication hole in the left crankcase half must have clean chamfered score free edges, if not the O ring on the retaining ring holder could be damaged when fitted.

Well grease the O Ring and retaining ring on the retaining ring holder. If the housing is still hot, press in the complete retaining ring holder until in position.

Remarks: Bearings or retaining rings in the absence of a pressing tool should only be driven in very carefully with a suitable punch. With a housing temperature of about 150° C the cold bearings in any case almost fall into their position by themselves.

Prepare both gear bearings and check on the correct fitting of the circlips in the casing and on the bearings. Press bearings in the casing from inside. When doing this take care to see that the bearings are not pressed too forcibly against the circlips because as a consequence they could become distorted.

Next the dimension from the casing sealing surface to the bearing plane surfaces is to be checked. This dimension in the case of left half section casing equals 88.9 mm. If the bearings are in too far then these have to be brought back to the correct position by tapping with a punch on the perimeter of the outer race.

If the bearings are not tightly seated after cooling (the hole in the casing must be at least 0.045 mm smaller than the bearing outer diameter) then it is to be considered that with heating in the casing they became distorted. In such a case the casing is to be replaced.

The butting faces of the controller drum of the catch lever and the control shaft must also have a distance of 88.9 mm from the casing joint faces.

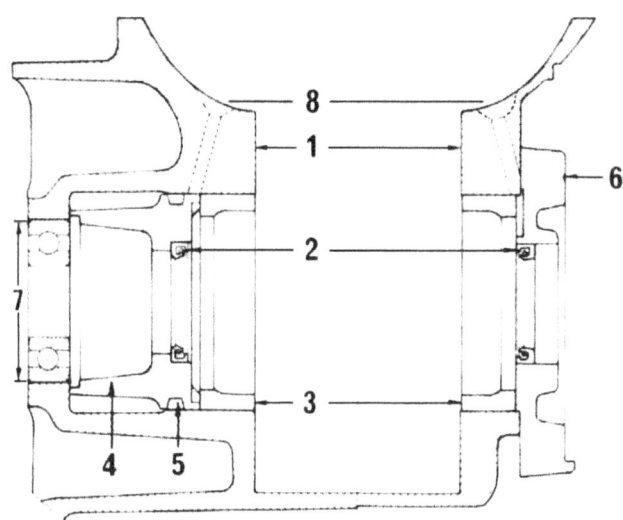

1 Crankcase
2 Retaining rings
3 Main bearing outer collars
4 Retaining ring holder
5 O-Ring
6 Sealing flange
7 Recommended diameter for drift used to press out grooved bearing.
8 Lubrication holes for main bearings

Right crankcase half

Heat the casing to 100–150° C and knock out the gear bearing by light tapping with the plastic hammer from the outside of the casing inwards. Remove retaining ring near the drive shaft.

To dismantle the main bearing outer race proceed as follows: Unscrew sealing flange with gasket and retaining rings. Press the race from the outside inwards. Fit sealing flange with new retaining ring and gasket. (Pay attention to correct position of the lubrication grooves). Press the new race in the still warm casing until it meets the sealing flange. Press in the gear bearing until it touches the circlip. After the casing has cooled down, check bearing is well seated in the correct position. The distance from the casing sealing surface to the bearing plane surface is equal to 36.9 mm on this side. If necessary adjust the bearing.

Fit new retaining ring on the transmission output driveshaft with packing washer fitted inwards.

Crankshaft pre-assembly

Remarks: As previously mentioned the ball race rings and ball cages of the main bearings must under no circumstances be mixed together.

Main bearings should only be renewed as sets, never singly.

Measuring of crankshaft axial play

If you renew the crankcase or the main bearings, the axial play of the crankshaft is to be measured. This must also be done if only removing the outer ring from the casing.

Place the engine casing halves with the inside facing upwards and place the ball cages with inner race rings in appropriate outer race rings in the casing. With the depth gauge, measure the distance from the casing joint face to the bearing inner race surface.

Make a note of measurement results and measure the second crankcase half. Add together both measurements and add to this 0.2 mm for the gasket.

Measure the crankshaft at the bearing contact surfaces and also make a note of those measurements.

The axial play, through different thicknesses of compensating shims between the crank web and the bearing inner race rings should be so arranged that there remains an axial play of about 0.03–0.05 mm.

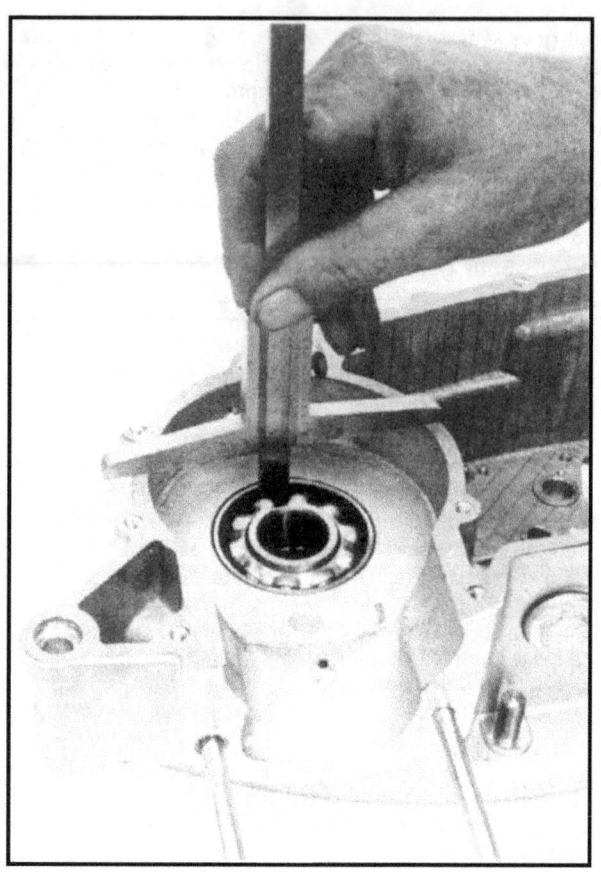

Example:

Left crankcase half	27.48 mm
Right crankcase half	+ 27.45 mm
Gasket	+ 0.20 mm
Measurement in Crankcase	= 55.13 mm
Measurement of Crankshaft	− 54.50 mm
Existing axial play	= 0.63 mm
Permitted axial play	− 0.03 mm
Equalising difference	0.60 mm

This difference on both sides of the crankshaft is adjusted by the compensating shims. If the axial play cannot be corrected with the same number (thickness) of compensating shims on both sides, then the larger number should be fitted on the clutch side. Press ball cages from the inner rings.

Before forcing on the inner race rings, in each case there is to be placed an intermediate plate between both crank webs. This intermediate plate must be large enough for support of both sides and thus the crank shaft clearly rests upon it (press on inner rings with inscription outside).

Never tighten the crankshaft with a crank shaft pin or on the frame in the vice and try to hit the bearing inner rings. In such a case the crank webs are squeezed together and the connecting-rod bearing is damaged which means the crankshaft cannot be used. After pressing on the inner rings fit the ball cage on the crankshaft.

Fix left half casing in the clamping frame; Oil the retaining rings and introduce the crankshaft. Fit the gasket and fix the right half casing with screws. Rotate the crankshaft. Check with dial gauge for lateral wobble at crankshaft ends. This must not exceed 0.05 mm on the driving as well as the magneto side. Measure the axial clearance of the crankshaft, holding a dial gauge against a crankshaft end. By pushing the crankshaft backwards and forwards several times it can be ascertained that it is free. If the axial play does not lie between 0.03 mm and 0.05 mm then the crankshaft must be dismantled and an inner ring is taken out by means of the inner ring extractor. Add or take away corresponding compensating washers.

Kickstart – Installation

Insert split pin for catch lever spring with washer, through the hole in the casing, from inside, push outer washer onto the split pin and bend over (It must fit tightly in the casing). Flatten the split pin head. Insert the catch lever before fitting it on the kickstarter shaft and check for ease of operation. Replace the spring on the catch lever (make sure the spring is in the correct position).

Note: Up from engine-No. 7-5506 243 crankshafts with 68 mm stroke are assembled on our 400 cc engines.
In case of doubt identifiable by the punched in number 68 (on both hubs of the crankshaft).

On the 400 cc engines crankshafts are assembled with fly-rings. When installing the fly-rings pay attention that those are glued with Omnifit type green 150 M and the allen flat head screws with Omnifit type red 80 M.

It is also possible to apply the corresponding equivalent products of LOCTITE.

After the glueing process the crankshaft needs a resting time of about 24 hours enabling the adhesive to harden.

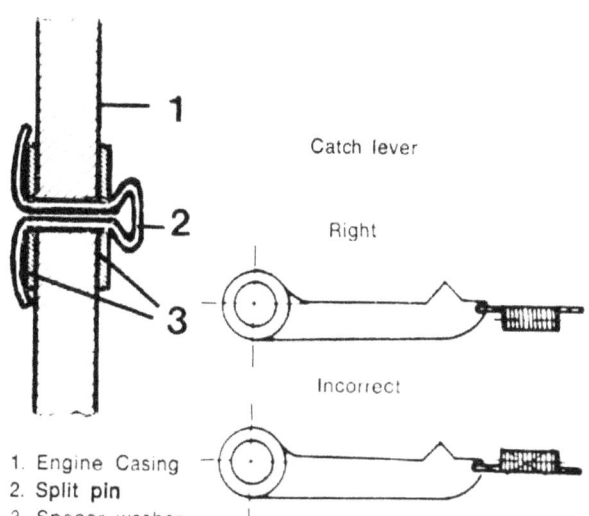

1. Engine Casing
2. Split pin
3. Spacer washer

Place kickstarter sprocket, thrust washer (only on kickstarter shafts with 14 mm diameter and kickstarter ratchet wheel in the casing. Rebend the spring support downwards near the hole on the right side (top view) so that the spring does not come out. Hook spring to spring support in the hole in the kickstarter ratchet wheel and insert. (In the case of models with starter shafts of diameter 14 mm replace in the first hole in clockwise direction).

Try the box screw on the kickstarter shaft and then give a good oiling to the kickstarter shaft and insert it from the inside through the casing. From above place on the locking plate with tongue. Centre the shaft and, tighten box screw with torque of 39.2 Nm (4 kpm). Fit kickstarter lever and tighten with a turn of about 1 1/4. Screw in the kickstarter stop screw with sealing ring and release the kickstarter lever. Check kickstarter sprocket for easy running and axial-clearance tolerance. Between the lateral gear tooth system of the kickstarter sprocket and the kickstarter ratchet wheel a clearance of at least 1 mm must be provided in the idling position.

If this is not so, then the axial clearance of the starter shaft must be checked. For adjustment of the axial clearance there are available several thicknesses of locking plates. The thinner the locking plate the smaller will be the axial clearance.

Remarks: In the case of the kickstarter stop screw there are two different types. The type A can only be used with engine model 51/52. Type B is used in model 54/55. Screws are easily identified by the shape of the head.

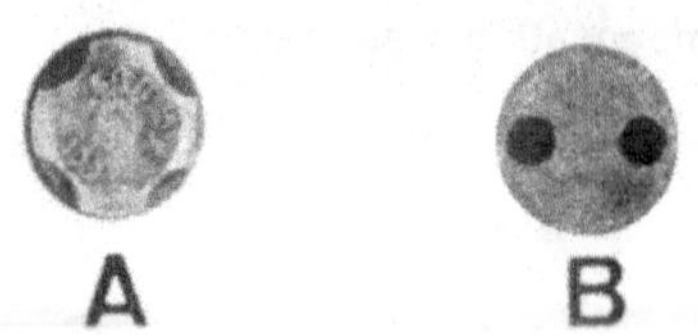

A   B

Secure locking plate in the lower casing slot with punch, bend tongue inwards and bend up and press against opposite side on the hexagonal.

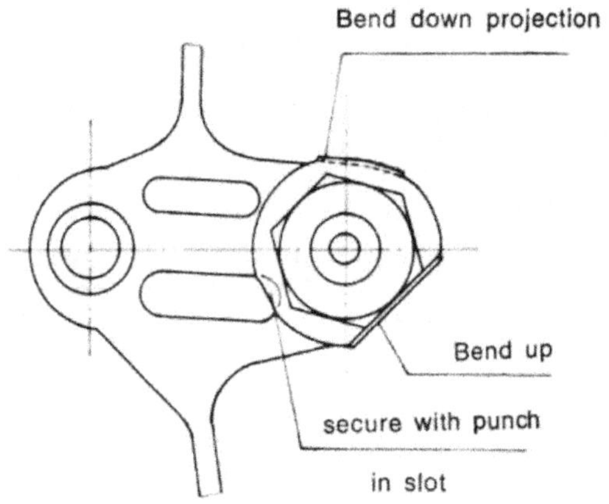

Bend down projection

Bend up

secure with punch

in slot

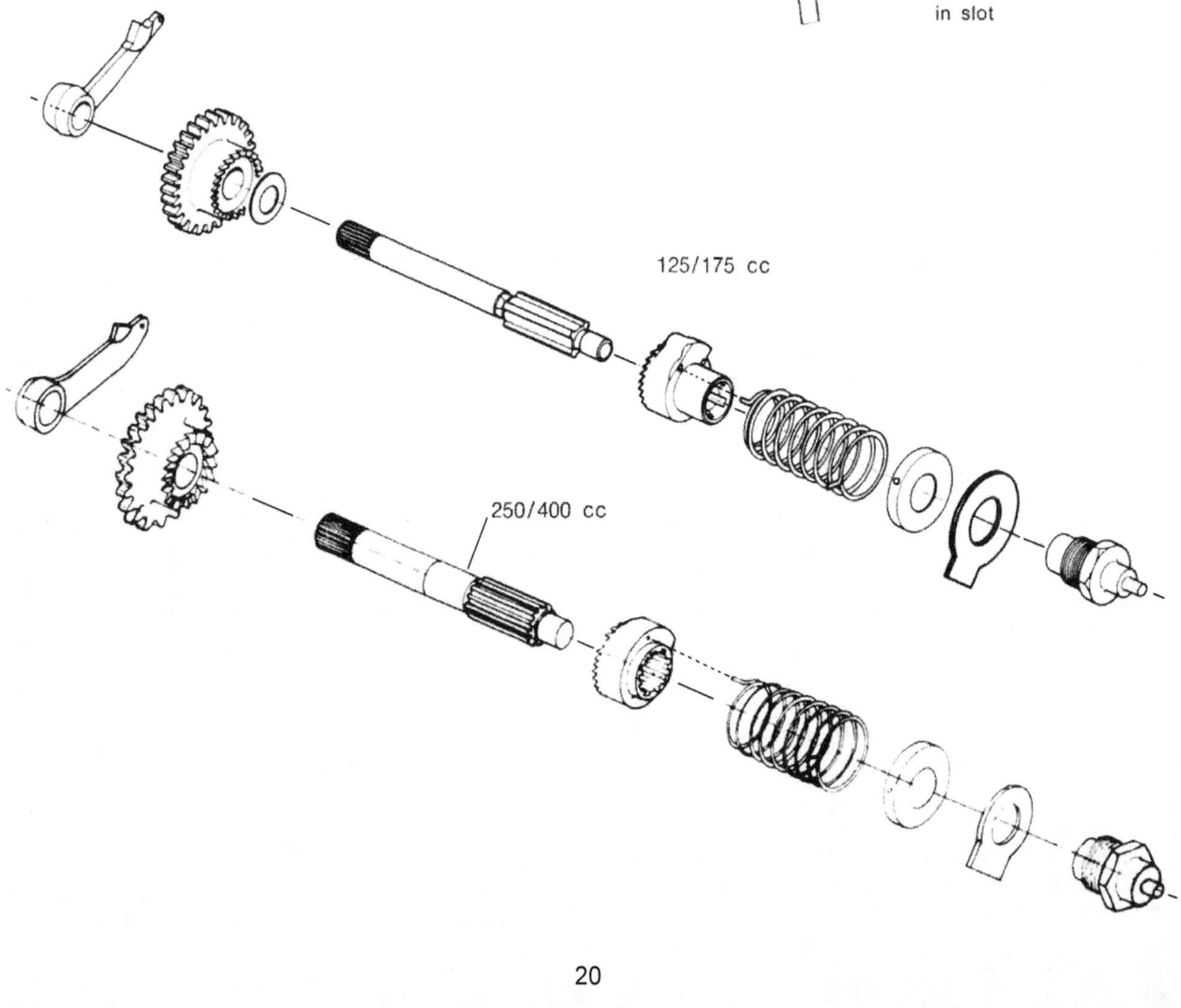

125/175 cc

250/400 cc

Transmission
Assembly instruction:
Check shafts for wear on the profile flanks where the needle cages run. Clean all holes. Tighten shafts with teeth underneath in the vice and between aluminium jaws. Fit all distance rings one after a another, needle cages, sprockets, thrust washers and retaining rings. Check used parts for wear.

Fit retaining rings with sharp edges always on the engine side and take care that they are not consequently over elongated (use special pliers). Loose sprockets kept between retaining rings should not have more than 0.2 mm axial clearance and also must not get jammed between the thrust washers.

Assembly of the driving shaft
First of all push distance sleeve (1) up to the 1st gear teeth cut from the shaft material. Fit the divided needle bearing cage (2) and above that the 2nd gear loose sprocket 3. with the shift dog of the 1st gear teeth turned off the shaft. Push the inner toothed thrust washer (4) (the smallest of the two) up to the 2nd gear loose sprocket. Fit the smaller of the two circlips (5) in the groove before the thrust washer in the 2nd gear loose sprocket and push on the shaft the 3rd/5th gear — sliding sprocket (6) with the smaller gear rim adjusted to the 2nd gear loose sprocket.

Fit the larger circlip (7) in the annular tee slot at the end of the grooved shaft section and push the larger inner toothed thrust washer (8) up to the stop. Fit the divided needle bearing cage (9) on the shaft and push over this the 4th gear loose sprocket with shift dogs adjusted to the 3rd and 5th gear loose sprocket. Then follows a distance sleeve (11) and the 6th gear fixed sprocket (12).

When changing the gear sprockets, special care must be taken to make sure number of teeth, i. e. the original coincides with the replaced parts.

When the thrust washer (13) has been fitted, pre-assembly of the driving shaft is completed.

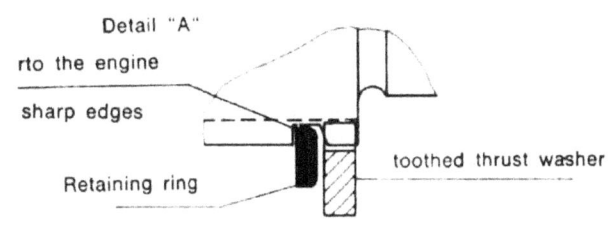

Detail "A"
rto the engine
sharp edges
Retaining ring
toothed thrust washer

6th Gear	28 Teeth (125. 175 Enduro 29 Teeth)
4th Gear	24 Teeth
5th Gear	26 Teeth
3rd Gear	21 Teeth
2nd Gear	18 Teeth
1st Gear	14 Teeth

Forged gear-wheels are identifiable by the milled groove

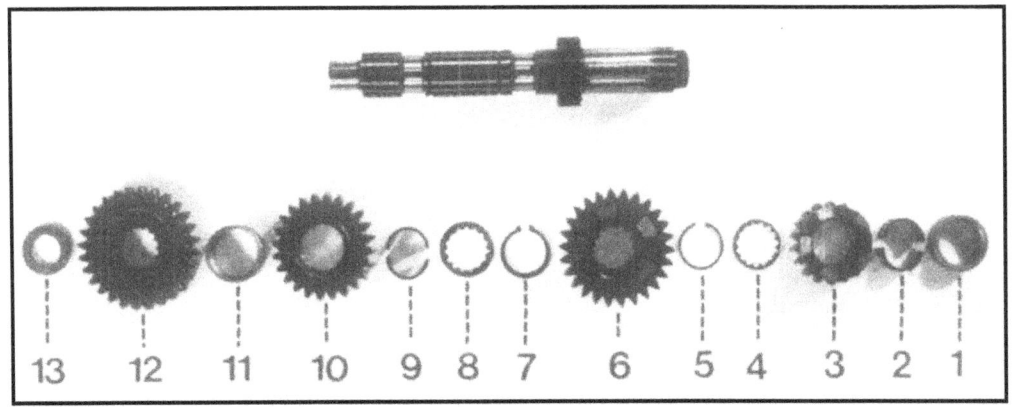

ATTENTION! In case of the 125/175 cc motor, two different transmissions are available for the sixth speed.
Type 1) 28:21 as for all other stroke volume categories
Type 2) 29:21

Assembly of the driven shaft

Push needle cage (2) up to the flange of the driven shaft. Push the 6th gear loose sprocket (3) over the needle bearing so that the shift dogs point away from the flange. Fit support washer (4) and circlip (5). Push 4th gear sliding sprocket (6) on the shaft in such a way that the shift fork groove is adjusted to the 6th gear loose sprocket. Fit circlip (7). Then push the inner toothed thrust washer (8) on the shaft clearing the circlip (the hole in the washer, when this is correctly seated in its groove, must pass over the circlip).

Next fit the divided needle bearing cage (9) on the shaft and the 5th gear loose sprocket (10) is to be pushed over the bearing in such a way that its shift dogs point to the 4th gear sliding sprocket.

Fit the 3rd gear loose sprocket (11) with shift dogs turned away from the 5th gear loose sprocket. Fit inner toothed thrust washer (12) and circlip (13).

Push on the shaft 2nd gear sliding sprocket (14) with its shift fork slot adjusted to the 3rd gear loose sprocket. Fit support washer (15) and needle bearing cage (16). Push on the 1st gear loose sprocket (17) with the smaller gear rim adjusted against the 2nd gear sliding sprocket. Fit thrust washer (18).

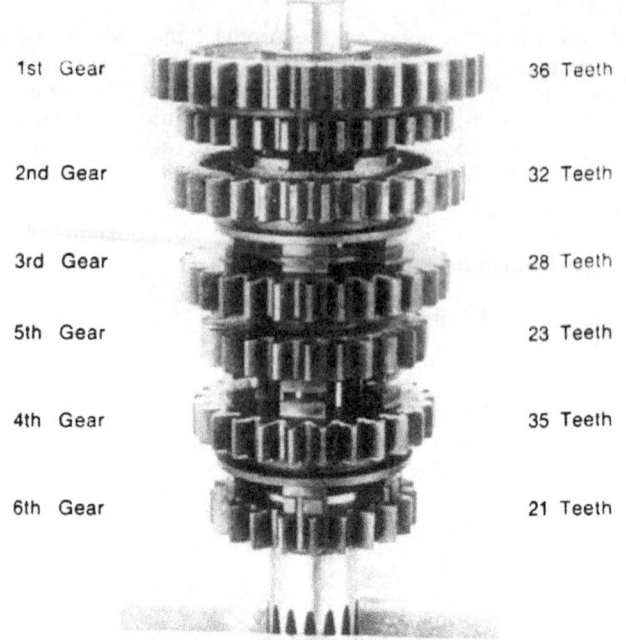

1st Gear	36 Teeth
2nd Gear	32 Teeth
3rd Gear	28 Teeth
5th Gear	23 Teeth
4th Gear	35 Teeth
6th Gear	21 Teeth

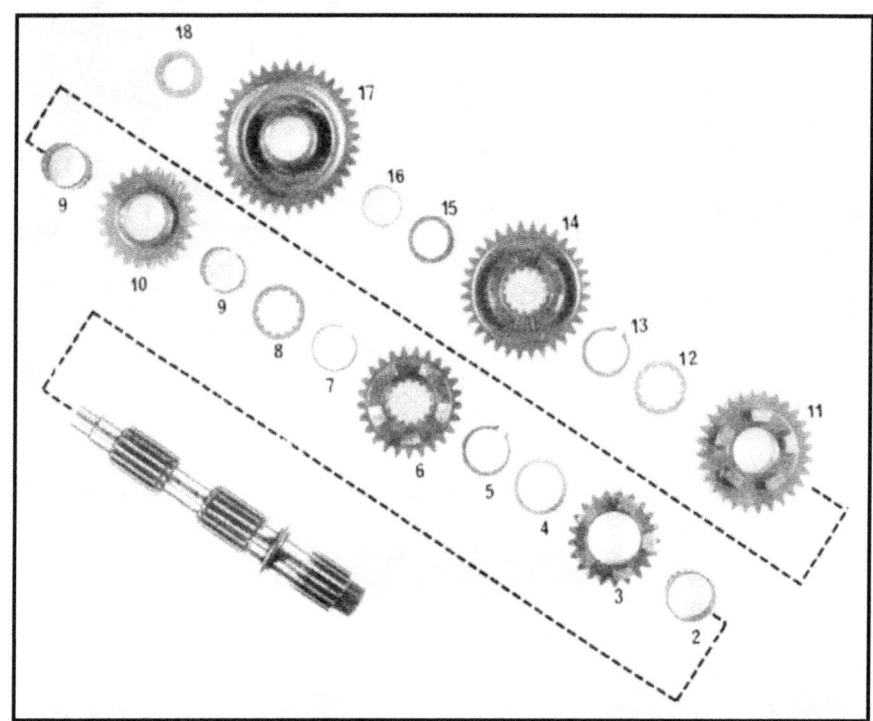

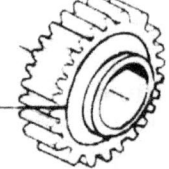

Forged gear-wheels are identifiable by the milled groove

Gear — shift

Check wear of gear shift forks on the gearing engagment position of the ratchet wheels and the controller barrel. It is to be checked also if the shift fork and shift rails are at an angle of 90° to each other and, if necessary, rebend.

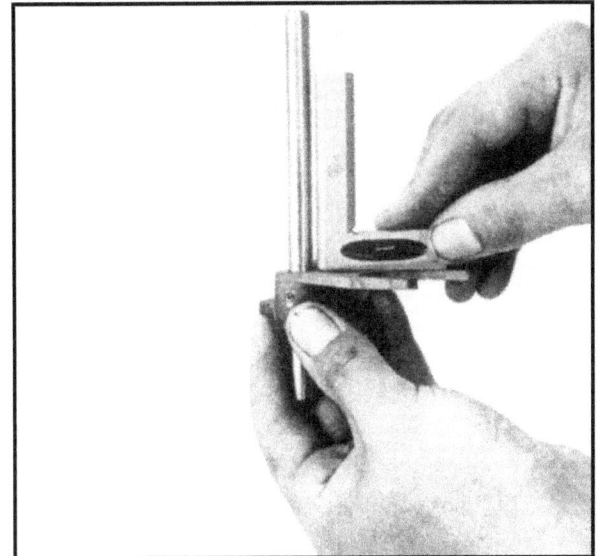

Check wear of gear shift unit (especially on the roundness which interlocks in the controller barrel). The distance between the front surfaces of the upper shift catch must not be greater than 54.8 mm but, if the distance exceeds this, then the shift unit must be renewed.

1. Shift spindle
2. Shift lever
3. Shift unit
4. Shift lever spring

After fitting the inner shift lever, on the shift spindle it is to be checked whether the shift lever and spindle are at an angle of 90° to each other. If necessary rebend lever.

When fitting the shift unit, pay attention to the correct positioning of the shift lever spring.

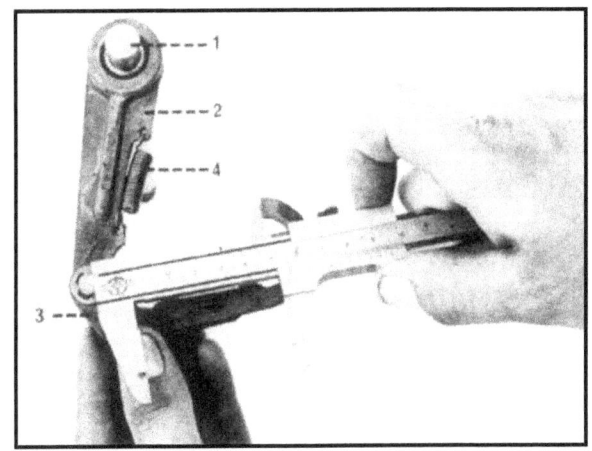

Difference between 5 gear (MC) and 6 gear enduro clusters

Both clusters are almost equal in make-up: The only difference lies in the fact that in the case of the 5 gear design the first gear of the 6 gear cluster cannot be engaged.

The 5- and 6-speed-drums are identifiable thereby, that on the 5-speed drum a longer steel pin is pressed in, which protracts 3 mm from the face (A).
When using the longer pin and the hexagon head screw with full dog point the first gear is locked.

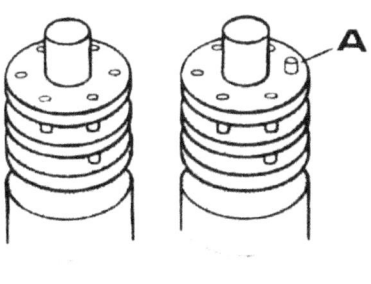

6 Gear   5 Gear

Exchange from 5-speed to 6-speed gearbox

Turn out hexagon head screw with full dog point (1), spare part-No. 0561 080303 (M8 × 30) and replace it by a hexagon head screw with full dog point spare part-No. 0561 080203 (M8 × 20).

Re-setting from 6-gear to 5-gear transmission

When re-setting from 6- to 5-gear care must be taken that neither first gear nor neutral is engaged. Otherwise the gear shift drum could be damaged near the locking-pin when the hexagon-head dog-point screw (M8 × 30) is introduced.

Clutch

Check for wear in clutch discs, clutch cage and clutch centre.
Check clutch cage bearing and in the case of excess play or considerable running noise, renew.
Clutch measurements:

Note:
Tue outer clutch hub can be delivered loose (without pinions). The fastening of the outer clutch hub with rivets must be carried out by a specialist.

Clutch measurements:

125/175:	Organic disc	2,75 mm
	Alu disc	1,50 mm
250:	Organic disc	2,75 mm
	Steel disc	1,50 mm
400:	Organic disc	2,50 mm
	Steel disc	1,00 mm

Lenths of clutch springs:

125/175: 1,5 mm diam. about 40,5 mm
250/400: 1,7 mm diam. about 37 mm

Installation sequence of clutch discs

- 125/175: Beginning with an organic disc you have to put in alternatively six organic and six ALu discs.
- 250: Beginning with an organic disc you have to put in alternatively seven organic and six steel discs.
- 400: Beginning with an organic disc you have to put in alternatively eight organic and seven steel discs.

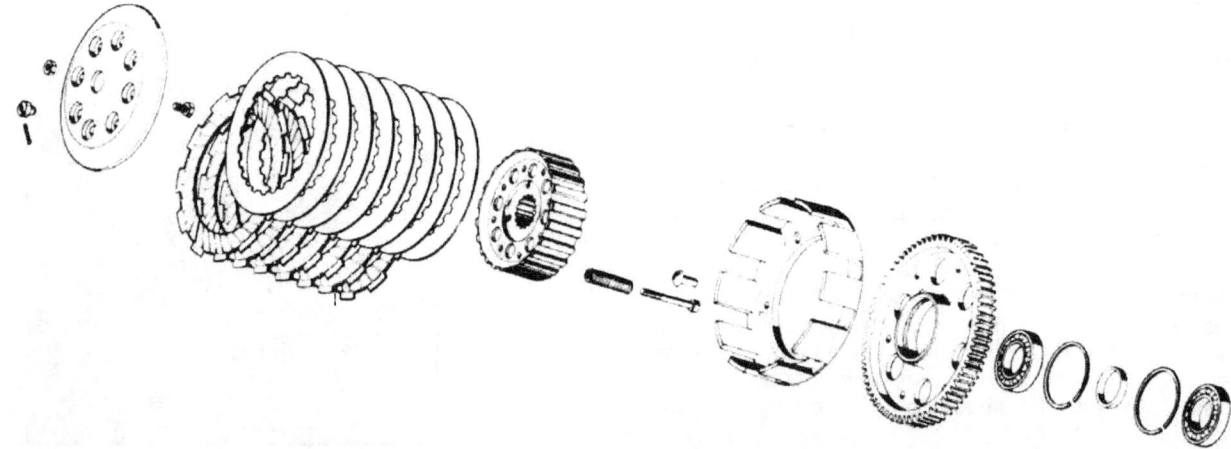

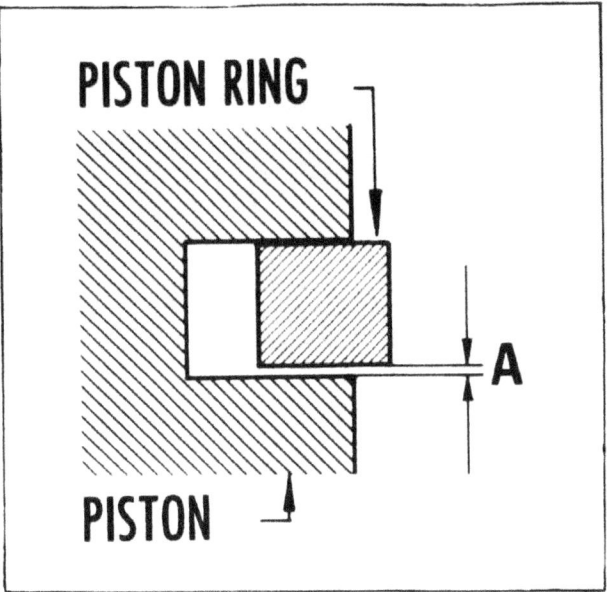

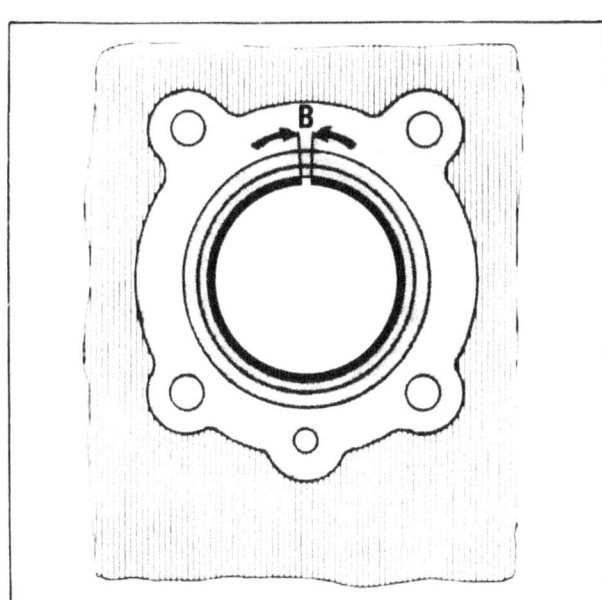

PISTON — PISTON RINGS

Piston

If a piston already used, is to be inserted again, the following points have to be examined:

1) Piston bearing surface: check for eventual pressure marks ("Seizing of the piston") slight friction marks may be eliminated by means of a fine emery stone.

2) Piston ring grooves: For this purpose the piston rings have to be mounted onto the cleaned piston, and by means of a feeler gauge the play A between piston ring and groove can be measured. If the play results greater than 0.1 mm, the piston has to be replaced.

3) The rotary locks for the piston have to have a tight fit within the piston.

Piston rings

For the piston rings, the bearing surface has to be controlled very thoroughly, too. In case of hard chromium-plated rings it has to be checked whether the chromium layer untorn respectively unbroken.

In case of molybdenum-coated rings, the coating has also to be scrutinized for eventual cracks.

Gap

Insert the piston rings into the cylinder and align with the piston. Now the gap B, which should be of 0,7 mm maximum, can be measured with a feeler gauge. If the gap is greater than this, pistons and cylinders should be checked for wear. If the wear of pistons and cylinders lies within the tolerances the piston rings can be replaced.

Check wear of pistons and cylinders

In order to assess wear of pistons and cylinders the diameters of the piston and cylinder are measured with a micrometer (check at several points in order to detect oval wear). If the difference between these two values is greater than the piston fitting clearance* + 0,04 mm the cylinder must be re-bored to the next size up.

* Piston fitting clearance-see technical data.

Engine Assembly

Fix the left crankcase half in the vice. Make sure the kickstarter unit is secure. Oil gear bearing.

Fitting the gear transmission:

Remove the thrust washer, 1st gear loose sprocket, needle bearing and supporting disc from the driven shaft; place and centre in right sequence in the casing above the bearing of the driven shaft.

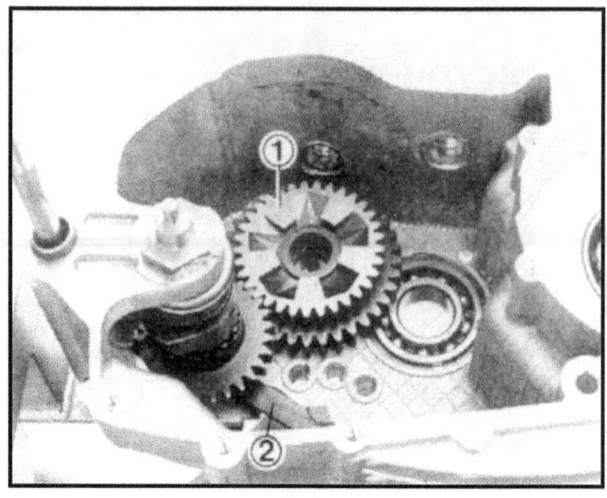

(1) Gear loose sprocket
(2) Catch lever

Mate driving and driven shaft together with the inserted shift forks with their sprockets set. Introduce both shafts into the casing in this position.

To facilitate assembly the 4th gear loose sprocket together with needle bearing, distance sleeve, the 6th gear fixed sprocket and the thrust washer can also be fitted later to the drive shaft.

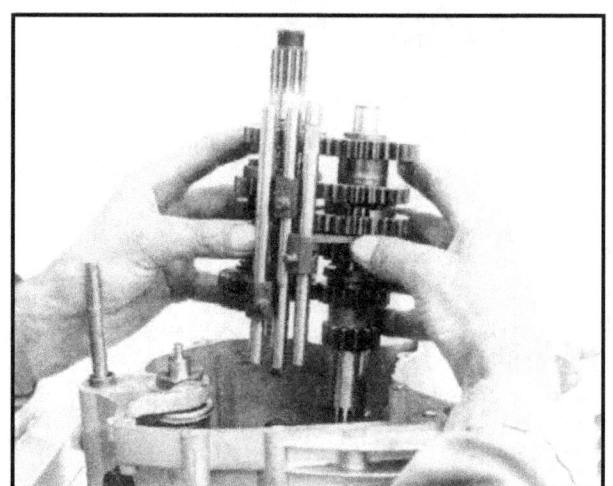

Gear change assembly

To install controller barrel, lift the shift forks of the 1st/3rd, 2nd/4th and 5th/6th gears one after another and place in corresponding slots of the controller barrel. The catch lever on the kickstarter shaft must now be pulled to the side, so that the controller barrel can be pushed in up to the transverse stop in the casing.

Introduce the sleeve for the controller barrel from below through the casing in the controller barrel, and screw up. Check if the catch lever in controller barrel is correctly rammed home.

Remarks: In the case of the 5 gear design, care should be taken that, before assembling the engine crankcase the 1st gear (fixed gear of the 6 gear transmission) is not, fixed as otherwise the gear unit cannot be shifted.

Remedial action: by turning the controller barrel.

Oil gear shift lever shaft and pass it through the casing. Insert the shifter unit in controller barrel. In particular pay attention to the fact that the return spring of the shift lever is replaced in the neck of the kickstarter box screw.

Now it must be possible to fully rotate the transmission without resistance. If shims were fitted on the gearshift lever shaft, these must be refitted.

Crankshaft

Place pre-assembled crankshaft in the left crankcase half.

Assembly of casing

Smear the sealing surfaces in the area, of the transmission with durable plastic sealing material and apply new gasket. Fixing of the gasket can be helped by use of grease in the area of the crank case.

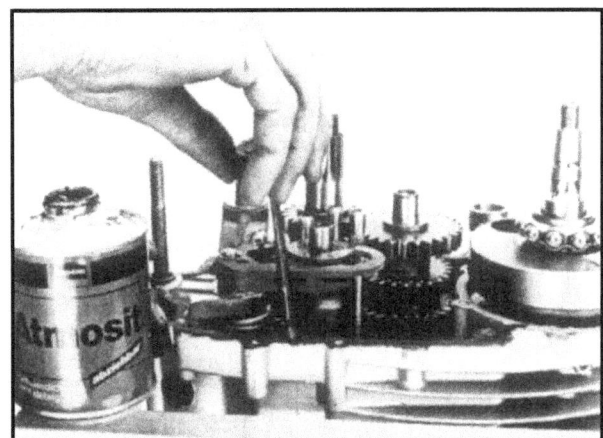

Make sure that both locating sleeves are seated on the left crankcase half. The 3 centering bolts are inserted on the shift rails. Fit on the right casing half. Centre gear shift lever shaft and controller barrel. Remove centring bolts.

Grease casing screws in the area of the thread and on the contact surface of the head. Fit screws and screw up the casing. Before tightening the screws check once again for easy movement with a torque of 6.9—7.9 Nm (0.7—0.8 kpm) on all shafts, as well as gear change unit.

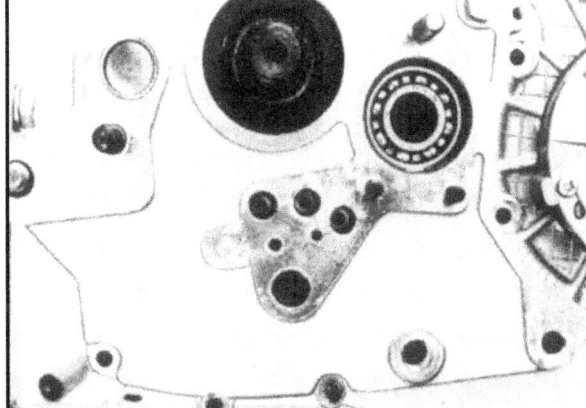

Checking of axial clearance of the transmission shafts

If axial clearance exceeds 0.1 mm, the clearance must be removed by replacing the small gear bearing.

Examination of the gear change unit:

Principle:

When a gear is fitted and the dogs placed in the bottom, the respective shift forks must not be subject to lateral pressure.

Fit all gears one after another through inspection hole by means of screwdriver, corresponding sprockets correctly mating with their dogs, pushed in such a way that the dogs are pushed against one another in the bottom. In this position the shift rails of the corresponding gears must have noticeable side clearance. This can be tested in the overhung ends of the shift rails.

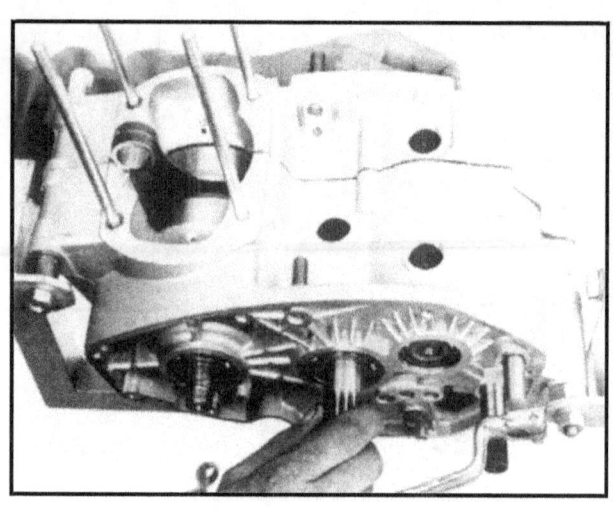

Primary drive clutch

Turn engine with clutch side upwards. Push downwards distance pieces with hollowed side on the crankshaft (only in the case of type 54/55). Heat crankshaft ball bearings to about 80° C and fit by use of the bearing extractor until they touch the crankshaft. Push supporting discs on the driving shaft and distance pieces on the crankshaft. Place clutch cage with bearings on the driving shaft. Fit driver with provisionally fitted screws, springs and nuts. Attach locking plate and nuts. Push clutch holder over the dog and kickstarter shaft. Tighten nut with torque of 68,7 Nm (7 kpm) and with punch locking plate inwards in the appropriate hole and press against a surface against nut.

Fit cotter in crankshaft and fit primary sprocket. Put on locking plate and nut. Tighten nut with 58.9 Nm (6 kpm) torque and make it secure.

Remove clutch holder and unscrew pring nuts. Starting with a facing disc alternatively fit facing and steel disc after one another (Page 24).

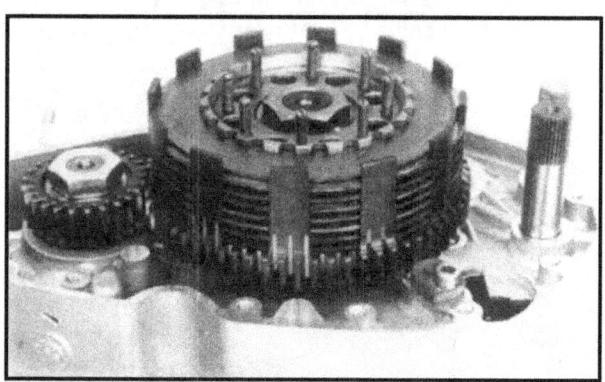

Clutch disengagement 250 and 400 cc

On 250 and 400 cc engines put push-rod* with pressure bearing support and bearing race into the main-shaft. Oil bearing race, put in ball bearing and mount pressure plate.

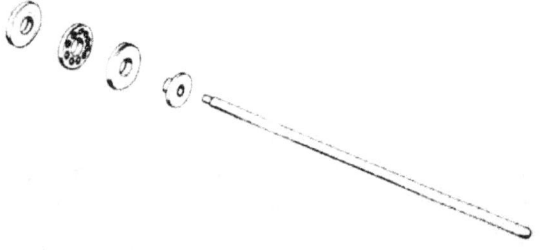

* Smear clutch pressure rod on both end with Molykotte paste

Put on pressure cap and with special screwdriver screw on spring nuts.

Pressure rod — 125/175 cc engine

Turn engine. Allow the clutch pressure rod* to fall with the rounded off end in driving shaft. Follow with the ball and second pressure rod.
*Smear clutch pressure rods on both ends with Molykotte paste.

Fitting of bearing cover

Smear sealing surface with sealing material. Put on gasket and bearing cover with O ring and tighten. Check disengaging lever and see if the measurement 44.5–45.5 from nipple base to the bearing cover is correct. If necessary adjust by bending the disengaging lever.

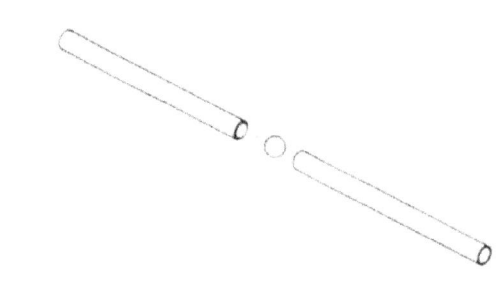

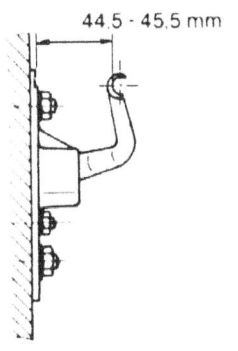

Distance with clearance O
44.5 - 45,5 mm

Turn engine in vice. Disengage clutch with disengaging lever and check if the pressure cap lifts up evenly. Centre the clutch by turning the springs nuts in both directions. Cotter the spring screws and seal with varnish.

Externally fit retaining rings to the clutch cover with packing washer. Smear sealing surfaces with durable plastic sealing material. Put on the gasket and fit cover. Grease screws and tighten with torque 6.9–7.9 Nm (0,7–0,8 kpm). After tightening the cover screws, test the kickstarter and the gearshift lever shaft for ease of operation.

Piston and Cylinder

When fitting new pistons pay attention to the sizes (1, 2, 3, 4) Additionally the lubrication hole for the exhaust stem is to be marked and drilled. For this reason it is necessary that the piston is fitted without piston ring (use auxiliary piston bolts).

Remove existing engine casing packing in the area of the cylinder base packing. Fit cylinder base packing and cylinder. Piston is placed in such a way that piston ring nuts in the upper area of the exhaust port are visible. Mark with a scriber, left and right in the piston, the stem in the exhaust port. Remove cylinder and take out piston.

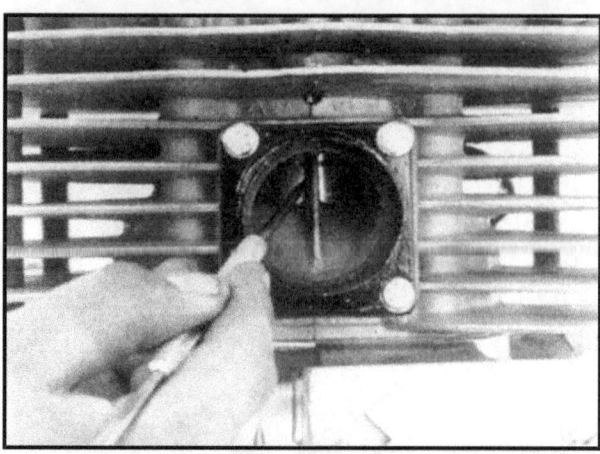

In the middle of both scratches about 8 mm from the lowest cylinder ring groove a hole of diameter 1.2 mm, to be drilled and trimmed.

After cleaning and oiling the piston and cylinder, fit both piston rings, heat piston, push needle bearing in connecting rod hole. When using new needle bearings, pay attention to the colour marking on the connecting rod and cage packing, fit gudgeon pin by using auxiliary gudgeon pin and fit gudgeon pin protection. Place piston on self-made wooden frame and adjust piston rings. Put on the cylinder and fix with 2 nuts.

Near the boss, the connecting rod has been marked with a red respectively blue coloured spot. Connecting rods with a blue marking have to be paired with needle cages the package of which is also marked in blue colour. Connecting rods with a red marking have to be paired with red marked cages.

Connecting rods with red marking may exceptionally be paired with blue coloured needle cages but this entails an increased play of the gudgeon pin bearing.

In no case connecting rods with blue marking are allowed to be paired with red coloured needle cages!

Adjustment of dimension "X"
(L Ring top edge – cylinder top edge in the case of T. D. C. positioning. Pistons with one piston ring: measure the difference between the upper edge of the piston and the upper edge of the cylinder.)

Obtain the prescribed measurement by placing different thicknesses of cylinder foot gaskets underneath.

> KTM Engine Type 51 – 125 cc
> 0.4 – 0.5 mm
>
> KTM Engine Type 52 – 175 cc
> 0.85 – 0.9 mm
>
> KTM Engine Type 54 – 250 cc
> 1.2 – 1.3 mm
>
> KTM Engine Type 55 – 400 cc
> 1.15 – 1.2 mm

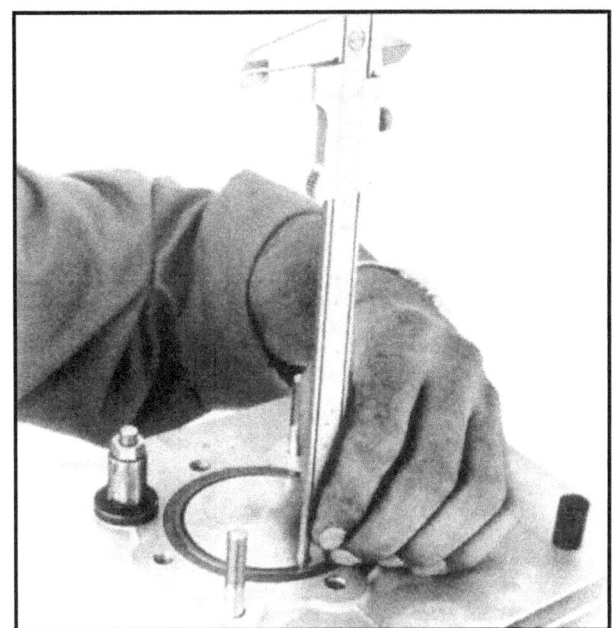

Take care when adjusting measurement "X". This is made by using cylinder base gaskets with various thicknesses.

If the dimension "X" is too great, compression is reduced and the engine loses power. On the other hand if the choice of the dimension "X" is too small the engine pinks and becomes overheated.

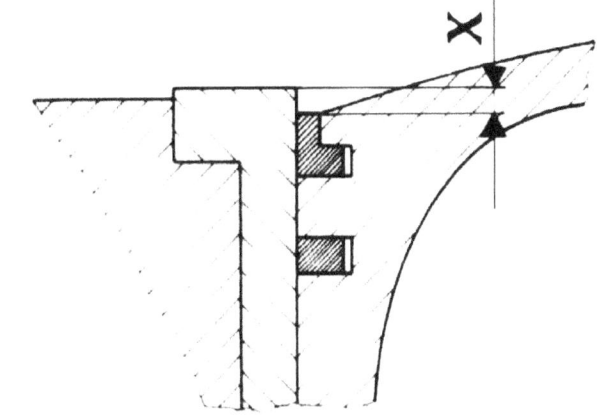

Cylinder head
Provisionally loosen screwed on nuts, clean sealing surface, put on the gasket. Oil the cylinder working surfaces with engine oil and put on the cylinder head. Tighten crosswise, screws and nuts with indicated torque (observe correct sequence). Always tighten the hexagonal screws first of all, so that the cylinder head is centred on the cylinder.

Chain wheel

Oil O Ring and push it over the driven shaft; push over the distance sleeve in such a way that the O Ring lays in the bevel. Fit chain wheel, locking plate and nut. Tighten chain wheel nut using the retaining spanner, torque of 49 Nm (5 kpm) (in no case exceed) and secure.

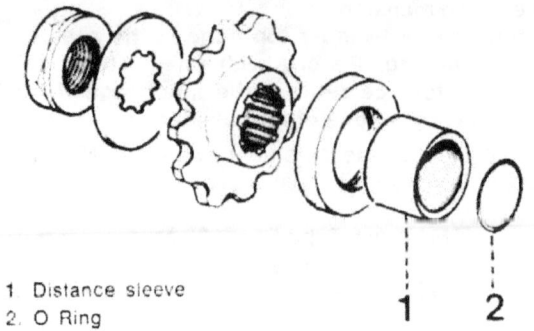

1. Distance sleeve
2. O Ring

Ignition System

Put cotter in crankshaft, fit baseplate on the sealing flange. Fix stator with 3 screws (do not tighten). Introduce cable lead correctly and fix it with retaining plates. Mount flywheel and fit spring washers with flange nut (do not tighten).

1. Stator
2. Hole for ignition adjustment

Ignition adjustment

Make sure the stator of the ignition system is loose (rotatable).

Screw in setting gauge for ignition point or dial gauge in spark plug thread. Introduce adjusting pin through the hole (2 mm) in flywheel and this is to be turned until the pin is well seated in the hole in the stator. Rotate flywheel together with stator to upper dead centre. Rotate flywheel with stator corresponding distance (pre-ignition) contrary to the direction of rotation of the engine. Pull the flywheel off with care (so that the stator is not further rotated).

Tighten the 3 stator fixing screws, tighten flywheel looking nut, torque 58,9 Nm (6 kpm)

Ignition point:

125	175	250
0,9–0,95 mm	1,9–2 mm	2,2 mm
BTDC	BTDC	BTDC

400
2,25–2,3 mm
BTDC

(1) Adjustment pin

Internal ignition installation

Fix stator with 3 screws (1) (not tighten), then install cable properly and fix it with the retaining plate. Put key in the crankshaft fix flywheel, mount spring washer with nut and tighten with 54–58.9 Nm (5.5–6 kpm)

Ignition adjustment (Internal ignition)

Screw in setting gauge for ignition point or dial gauge in spark plug thread.
Turn flywheel up to TDC and then turn back to the corresponding measurement (ignition advance) in oposite direction. After this turn stator until the timing marks will match and tighten the 3 stator screws.

Filling with Oil

Make sure that all drain plugs and regulating screws are tight. Fill with 1,6 litres engine oil SAE 20 or ATF oil and tighten locking screws with gaskets. Screw in vent plug in the rear hole.

A O Ring
B PVC distance collar

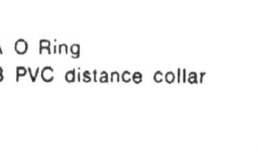

Fitting of gearshift lever and kickstarter

Several complaints in connection with broken engine casings in the area of the kickstarter stop screw are to be attributed to the fact that the gearshift lever and kickstarter have been wrongly fitted.

In connection with the kickstarter levers of new design, only shift gear lever can be fitted where the setscrew can be screwed from underneath upwards.

Push O Ring on kickstarter shaft. Oil and fit PVC distance collar. Fix kickstarter lever so that this has sufficient distance from the shift lever in idle position.

Oil check – Oil change

To check the oil, warm up the engine and tilt the machine over at an angle of 7°. This is necessary as the gear oil has been increased from 1,2 to 1,6 l.
Remove oil check screw under kickstarter shaft. If no oil comes out, add SAE 20 Motor Oil or ATF Oil until it shows at the check screw.
An oil change should be made at least twice annually. Naturally also, in this case the engine is warmed up. The machine is again placed in horizontal position. Having removed the oil drainage plug let the old oil drain away. Replace the oil drainage plug. Then refill through an oil filler plug with 1,6 litres engine oil SAE 20 or ATF oil. Fit screw plug with sealing ring.
Let engine run and check there are no leaks

(1) Oil check screw

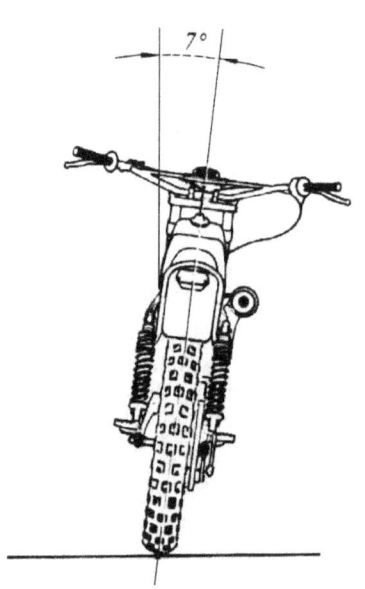

Wiring scheme for ignition and lighting system

Remarks: All KTM cross country sport machines are fitted with an electronic, magneto ignition generator without contacts (Motoplat).

The particular advantages compared with contact controlled magneto ignition generators are:

Increased certainty of operation, as there are no wearing parts such as contact breaker and greasing felt and the equipment together with the externally situated ignition coil, above all, is not affected by dampness and dust and completely free of maintenance.

Checking of the electronic magneto ignition generator must not be carried out with conventional testing equipment. Such test methods upset the system.

If the stator is damaged, both stator and flywheel should be replaced. Exchange ignition systems are available from KTM (not applicable to internal ignition) on the condition that the defective ignition equipment is sent to KTM. If the flywheel is in good condition this will be taken into account for the price of the exchange ignition system.

Attention: In no case must the plug cable be disconnected to switch off the engine.

To check the ignition spark, the high voltage cable must be connected to earth at all times. Preferably through a sparking plug (spark gap about 7 mm).

To facilitate removal or refitting of the equipment, at no time must the electronic cable (blue and black), which leads out of the stator, be cut for subsequent reconnection with a connecting block.

Here there exists the danger that through dirt and dampness on the exposed terminals short circuiting can lead to disturbance of the electronics.

The ignition coil must have faultless earth connection to the chassis. The contact faces should be clean. Attach, possibly, toothed washers or fit solid-type cable.

WIRING DIAGRAMME GS 80 GB, S, NL, SF

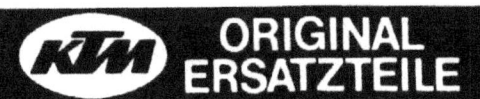

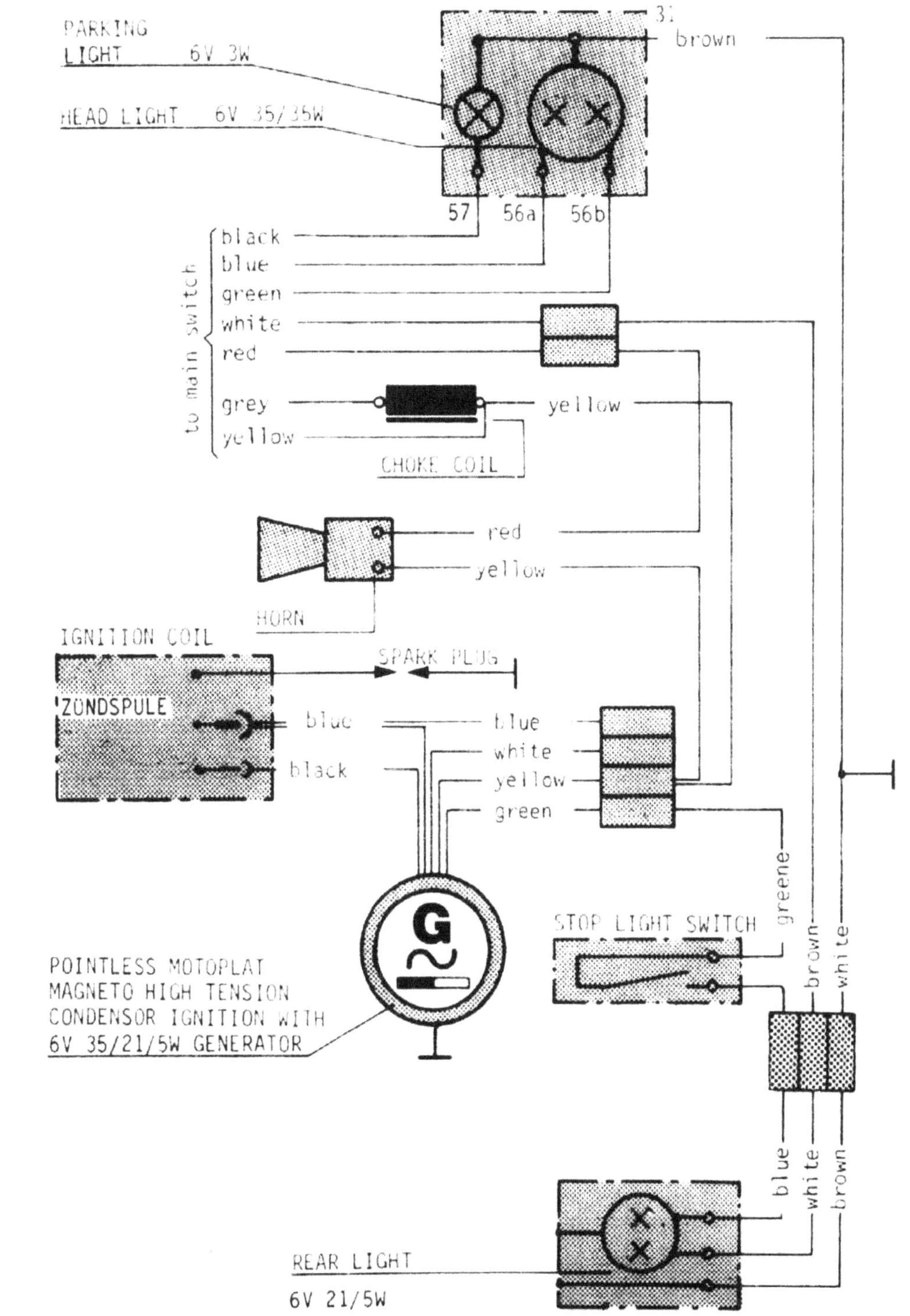

Carburettor

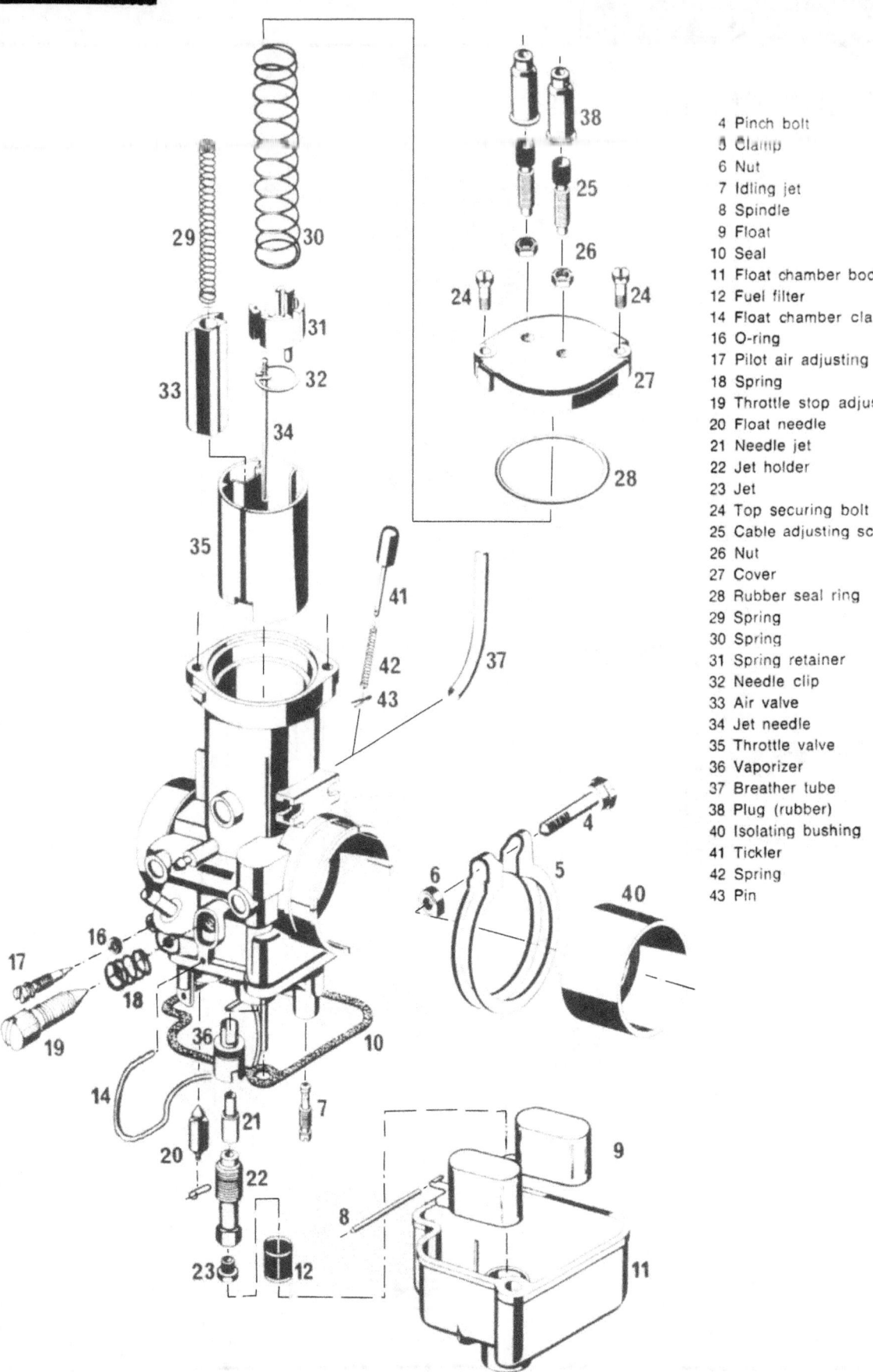

4 Pinch bolt
5 Clamp
6 Nut
7 Idling jet
8 Spindle
9 Float
10 Seal
11 Float chamber body
12 Fuel filter
14 Float chamber clamp
16 O-ring
17 Pilot air adjusting screw
18 Spring
19 Throttle stop adjusting screw
20 Float needle
21 Needle jet
22 Jet holder
23 Jet
24 Top securing bolt
25 Cable adjusting screw
26 Nut
27 Cover
28 Rubber seal ring
29 Spring
30 Spring
31 Spring retainer
32 Needle clip
33 Air valve
34 Jet needle
35 Throttle valve
36 Vaporizer
37 Breather tube
38 Plug (rubber)
40 Isolating bushing
41 Tickler
42 Spring
43 Pin

Carburettor Adjustment

Terms:

Too rich a mixture: Proportion of fuel too high in relation to the air.

Too weak a mixture: Proportion of fuel too low in relation to the air.

Idle running range: Running with closed slide valve.

Transition: Behaviour of the engine when opening the slide valve.

Part throttle range: Running when slide valve partly opened.

Full throttle range: Region when slide valve opened (ful gas).

Pinging: light metallic knocking in rhythm with engine rotation, caused through uncontrolled sudden combustion due to a too weak fuel/air mixture, a too high compression, a too low heat value of the plug, a too early ignition point or even gas leakages in the crank chamber.

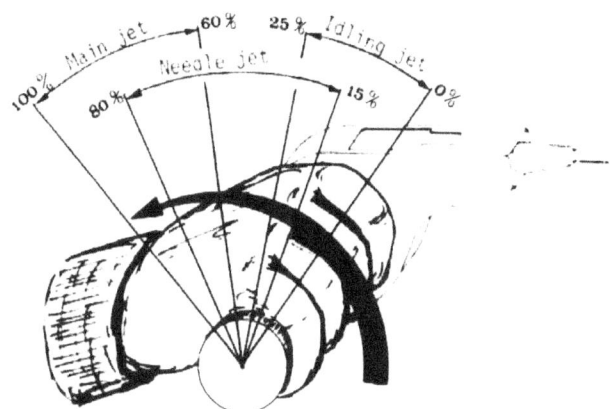

Principles

The original carburetter tuning is set for altitudes of between 300 and 400 m above sea level, medium temperature conditions (18%C), mainly cross-country use, middle-European Super petrols (ROZ 98 – MOZ) and a mixture of oil and petrol in the ratio shown on p. 4 (Mixture Ratio). Basic requirements are clean filter equipment and complete exhaust system. If the engine does not run without trouble under the conditions mentioned, first of all mechanical faults are to be looked for, the sparking plugs and ignition system to be checked.

If the carburettor setting for any reason is altered so that the fuel/air mixture becomes weak, pregeed with raution to avoid overheating and piston seizure.

Cross Country:
Idle running range — Adjustment

Screw in the valve regulating screw enough for the engine to have enough idling gas, then with mixture adjusting screw obtain the best possible even and steady running of the engine, then screw back the valve regulating screw enough to let the motor continue running smoothly without stopping. Check adjustment in semi-hot and hot condition.

Part throttle range

This is mainly influenced by the position of the needle. In the lower range it influences the idle running setting and in the upper the main jet influences the optimal part throttle setting. If the engine in the four stroke cycle or with partially throttled power runs in the case of acceleration with partially opened slide valve, the jet needle must be lowered a notch. If the engine pinks, especially when the engine is in the speed range of full power, the jet needle must be raised when accelerating.

If the phenomena described above should occur in lower part-throttle range they are to be rectified in the case of four stroke running by unscrewing the mixture regulating screw, in the case of pinging, to be rectified by screwing in the regulating screw. (in stages of half a turn).

(1) Mixture adjusting screw
(2) Valve regulating screw

Change over (Transition)

If the engine, in spite of better idle running and partial throttle adjustment when valve is opened, starts faltering and hunting and receives full power in bursts and with high revs., in most cases the fuel level is too high or the float valve is loose.

If in spite of satisfactory carburettor adjustment there cannot be obtained smooth idle running and smooth transition, the fault lies in the mechanical part (Cylinder, pistons, retaining ring, gaskets or in the ignition system).

Full throttle range

If the engine pings with full throttle or if after about 5 kilometres of full throttle running the insulator of a new sparking plug is very light or white then the main jet must be replaced with a larger one. If the insulator is dark brown or sooty, only after trying to find a mechanical reason and checking the filter for dirt, may a smaller jet be used. According to experience a smaller jet is only necessary in high altitudes i. e. very low air pressure.

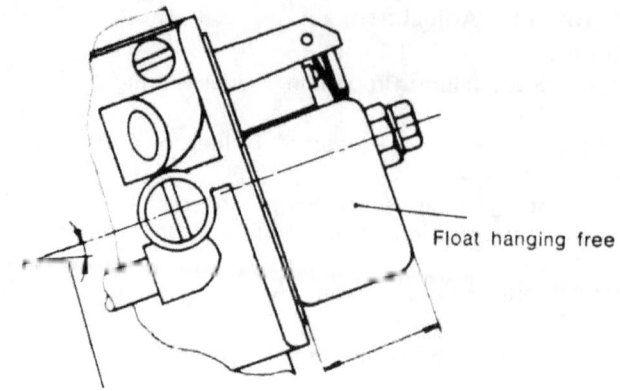

Float hanging free

Tilt about 15 degrees

Mixed Running

An engine, which is regulated for cross country or extremely high altitudes, runs too weakly on the highway or low altitudes, it pings and runs too hot. In this case the air valve must in each case be closed far enough to stop the pinging and there occurs a noticeable reduction of power.

If you drive with pinging engine, the cylinder and piston temperature will rise very quickly and the pistons will seize.

Running on the highway

The carburettor adjustment is the same as for cross country, but the idle running range can be kept somewhat richer. (Mixture regulating screw in). The part throttle range is to be regulated for richer mixture i. e. the jet needle is to be a notch higher. The full throttle range must be adjusted with the main jet for high altitudes. In nearly all cases the original main jet is optimal.

Air filter

The air filter element must be cleaned after each MC or cross-country race, or alternatively according to the amount of dust.
Wash the expanded plastic filter in clean petrol or a similar medium and dry well. Oil the filter element. (If possible, use FINA, TWIN AIR or BEL-RAY Filter Oil). When assembling the air filter element care must be taken that the expanded plastic filter is properly engaged over the filter retainer at the upper edge after insertion into the filter casing. (It can shift during insertion into the filter casing and then no longer seals properly.)

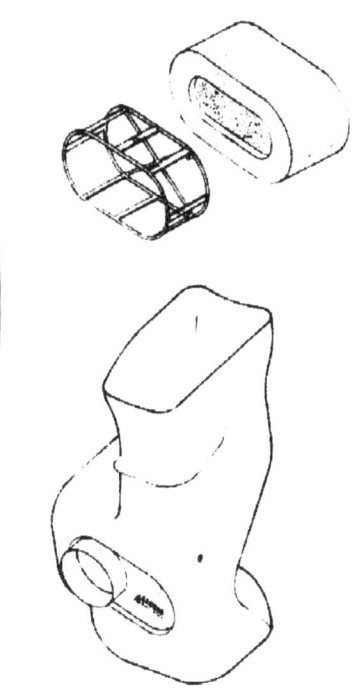

Adjustment of clutch cable

The clutch lever should have a clearance of about 15 mm measured from outside. If necessary correct with the regulating screw on the engine

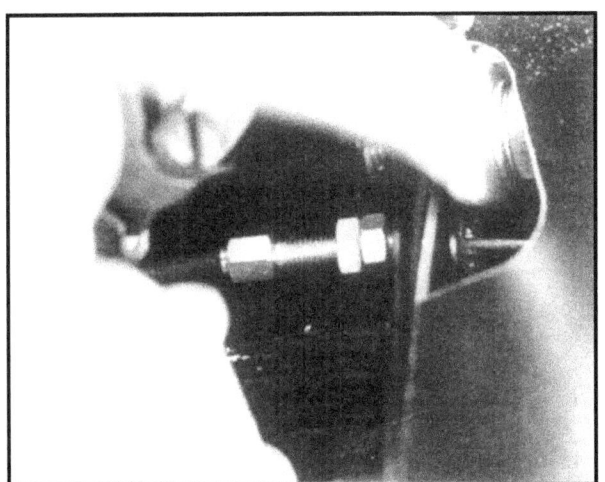

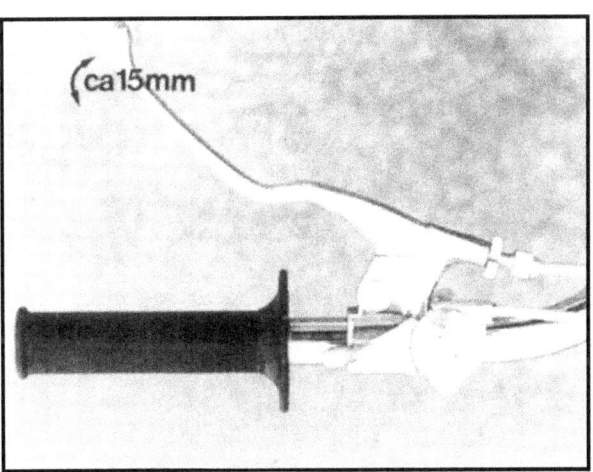

Lubrication and maintenance programme

Cylinder bore crank assembly
By mixture lubrication: Special 2-stroke oil mixed with fuel.
Mixture ratio: VALVOLINE 2 cycle competition oil SAE 40 1:40
CASTROL Super two stroke oil 1:25
BEL-RAY MC-1 Two cycle racing lubricant 1:50

Transmission
1,6 litres engine oil HD 20-30 or ATF oil.
Oil change after about 2.000 kilometres or after 2 race entries.
Check oil before every race entry.

Drive chain
If necessary remove chain, clean in petroleum and dip in hot chain grease or oil.

Cable
Teflon lined cables are standard equipment on KTM motorcycles. The only exception is the air regulating cable of GS models. Check ease of operation from time to time. Buckled or damaged cables should be replaced. Oil air regulating cable. DO NOT OIL LINED CABLES!

Air filter
Clean and oil, or even change, filter element before and/or after each race (if possible use FINA, TWIN-AIR or BEL-RAY filter oil). Check filter container and suction sleeve for tightness and clean also.

Fuel system
Twice annually empty fuel tank, clean fuel taps and examine fuel pipe line. If necessary clean carburettor, check parts for wear and renew gaskets.
Adjust carburettor.

Clutch adjustment
Continuously check clearance on clutch lever and if necessary adjust.

Ignition system
Check tight fit of terminals of the ignition system to the ignition coil and on the terminal strip. In the case of likelihood of water penetration the terminals of the ignition coil are sealed with silicon rubber, examine ignition timing at least every 2.000 kilometres.

Trouble shooting

Engine fails to start

CAUSE	REMEDY
Failure to run	Open fuel tap
	Replenish fuel
Fuel line blocked	Clean fuel taps, pipes and tank
Electrode distance too great	Rrduce distance
Plugs fouled by oil, wet or bridged	Clean plugs or renew
Ignition wire or plug connector damaged	Repair ignition wire and connector
Spark too weak	Examine ignition system
Water in the carburettor and jets blocked	Dismantle and clean carburettor

Engine without idle running

CAUSE	REMEDY
Idling regulation screw out of adjustment	Re-adjust idle running or replace idle running regulation screw
Ignition system damaged	Examine ignition system

Engine has not enough power

CAUSE	REMEDY
Basalt rock wool not sufficiently compressed or charred in silencer or secondary silencer	Add rock wool or renew filling.
Engine and exhaust equipment covered with carbon	Decarbonise engine and exhaust equipment
Air filter obstructed	Clean or renew filter cartridges
Fuel supply partly interrupted or carburettor blocked	Blow through fuel pipe and clean carburettor
Engine acquires secondary air through loose connections or poor gaskets	Tighten intake connections, if necessary, renew gaskets
Engine has too much retarded ignition	Check ignition
Compression loss through loose sparking plug, loose cylinder head or defective cylinder head gasket	Replace sparking plug and cylinder head or cylinder head gasket

Engine revs not high and running with four stroke cycle

CAUSE	REMEDY
Carburettor overflows if level adjusted too high, float needle seating is dirty or enlarged	Clean carburettor, if necessary, replace float needle and adjust level
loose carburettor jets	Tighten jets

Engine pings with full throttle

CAUSE	REMEDY
Carburettor regulation too weak	Adjust carburettor
Engine becomes too hot if cooling ribs on cylinder and cylinder head are very dirty	Clean cylinder and cylinder head
Engine has too much advanced ignition	Adjust ignition
Dimension "X" was incorrectly adjusted after fitting of cylinder and consequently compression too high	Correct dimension "X" by placing different cylinder foot gaskets underneath

Engine splutters into the carburettor

CAUSE	REMEDY
Lack of fuel	Clean fuel pipes, examine tank aeration and clean carburettor
Sparking plugs with incorrect heat value (Ignition by incandescence)	Fit correct plugs
Engine sucks in incorrect air	Tighten cylinder and carburettor screws, if necessary replace gaskets.

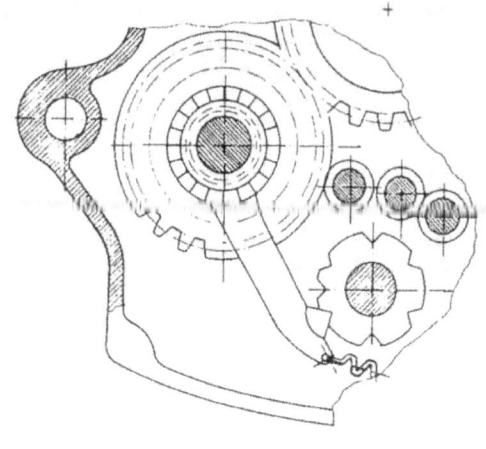
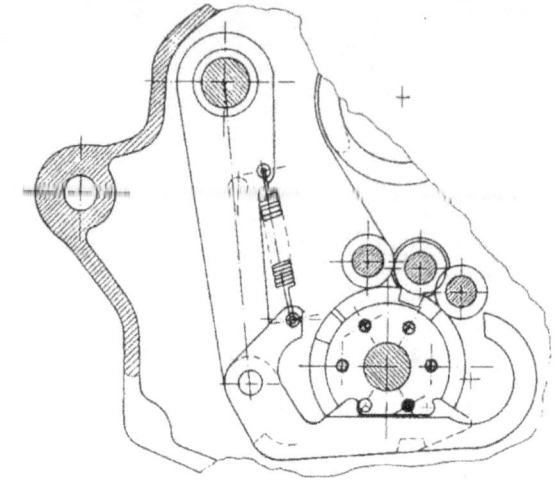
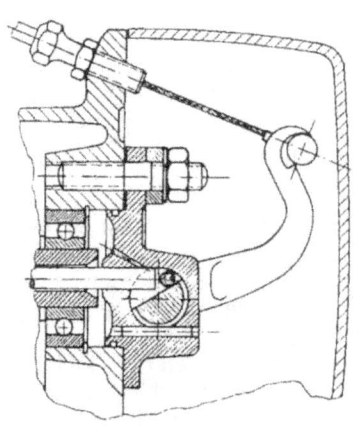
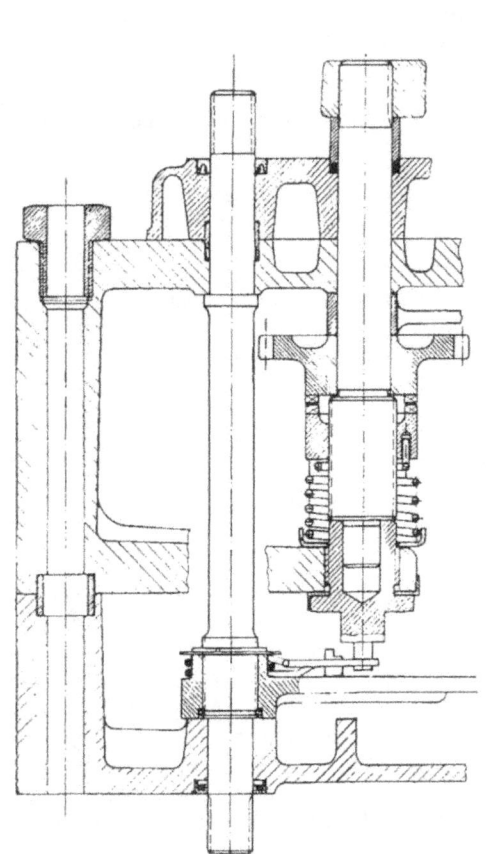
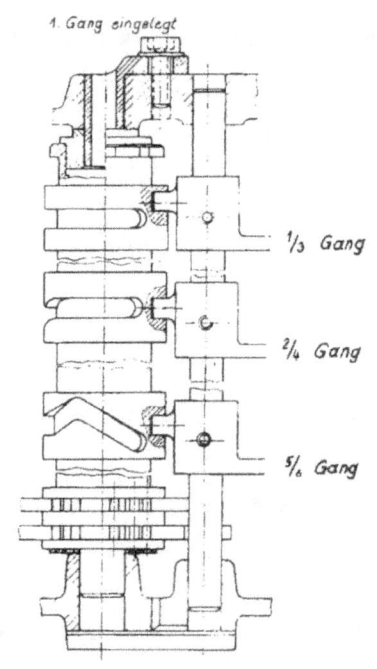

1. Gang eingelegt

1/3 Gang

2/4 Gang

5/6 Gang

NOTES

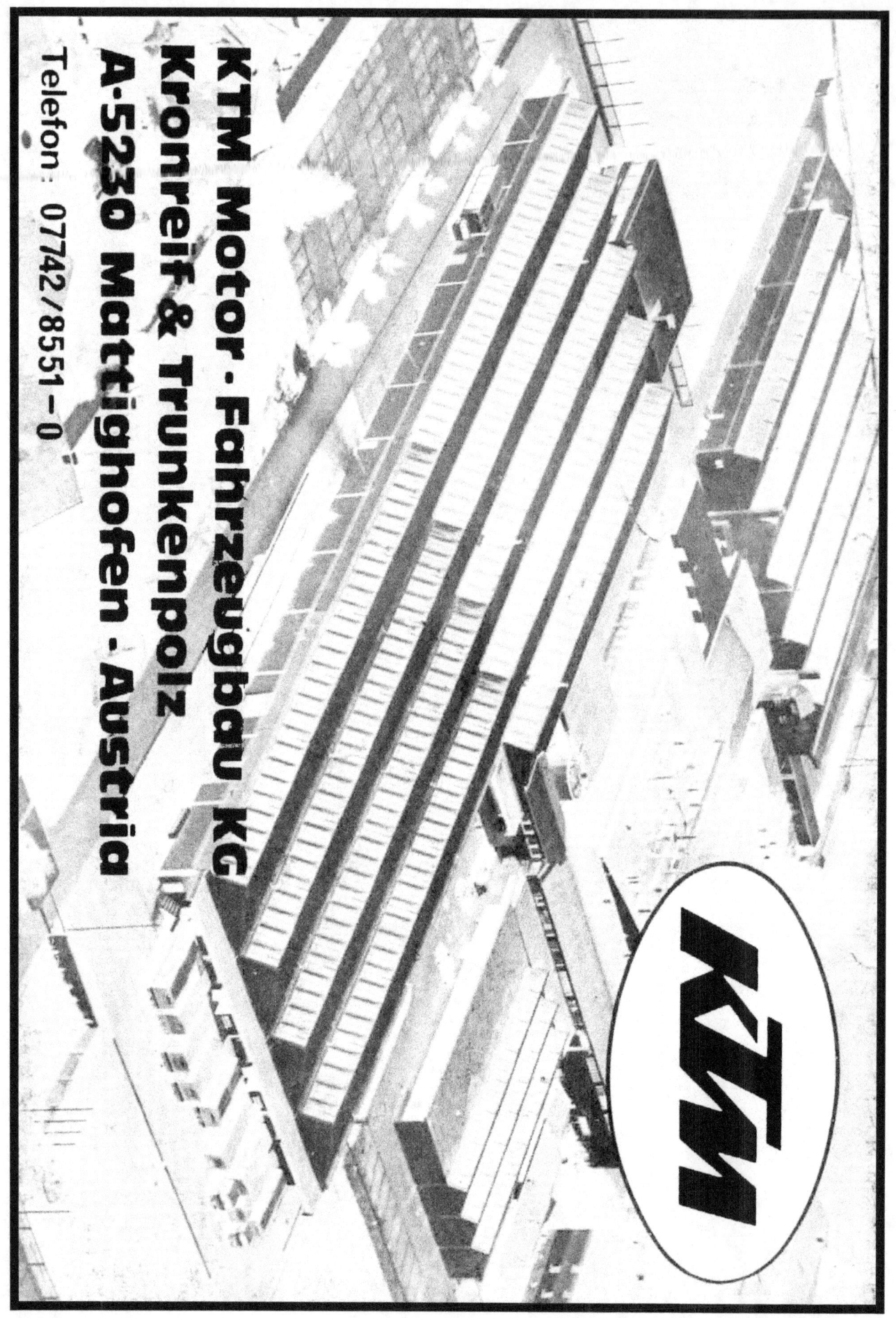

KTM

Parts list

**Engine 125
175
250
400 cc**

PREFACE

TRADEMARKS & COPYRIGHT

Penton® and KTM® are the registered trademarks of Penton, Inc. and Pierer Mobility AG. This publication is not sponsored by or endorsed by the trademark owners. We recognize that some words, model names and designations, for example, mentioned herein are the property of the trademark holder. We use them for identification purposes only. This is not an official publication however; it may include non-copyright works of the trademark holder.

INTRODUCTION

Welcome to the world of digital publishing ~ the book you now hold in your hand was printed using the latest state of the art digital technology. The advent of print-on-demand has forever changed the publishing process, never has information been so accessible and it is our hope that this book serves your informational needs for years to come. If this is your first exposure to digital publishing, we hope that you are pleased with the results. Many more titles of interest to the classic automobile and motorcycle enthusiast, collector and restorer are available via our website at www.VelocePress.com. We hope that you find this title as interesting as we do.

NOTE FROM THE PUBLISHER

The information presented is true and complete to the best of our knowledge. All recommendations are made without any guarantees on the part of the author or the publisher, who also disclaim all liability incurred with the use of this information.

INFORMATION ON THE USE OF THIS PUBLICATION

This manual is an invaluable resource for those interested in performing their own maintenance. However, in today's information age we are constantly subject to changes in common practice, new technology, availability of improved materials and increased awareness of chemical toxicity. As such, it is advised that the user consult with an experienced professional prior to undertaking any procedure described herein. While every care has been taken to ensure correctness of information, it is obviously not possible to guarantee complete freedom from errors or omissions or to accept liability arising from such errors or omissions. Therefore, any individual that uses the information contained within, or elects to perform or participate in do-it-yourself repairs or modifications acknowledges that there is a risk factor involved and that the publisher or its associates cannot be held responsible for personal injury or property damage resulting from the use of the information or the outcome of such procedures.

WARNING!

One final word of advice, this publication is intended to be used as a reference guide, and when in doubt the reader should consult with a qualified technician.

INDEX

GROUP	DESCRIPTION	PAGE
30 A/1	Crankcase I	2
30 A/2	Crankcase II	6
30/B	Crankshaft, Piston 125/175	10
30/B	Crankshaft, Piston 250/400	14
30/C	Cylinder 125	18
30/C	Cylinder 175	20
30/C	Cylinder 250/400	22
31	Carburator 125 GS/MC	26
31	Carburator 125 GS/Z	30
31	Carburator 175	34
31	Carburator 250	38
31	Carburator 400	42
31	Ignition	46
32	Clutch	48
33	Kickstarter 125/175	52
33	Kickstarter 250/400	54
33/I	Transmission I	56
33/II	Transmission II	58
34/I	Shifting Mechanism I	62
34/II	Shifting Mechanism II	64

GROUP 30A/1

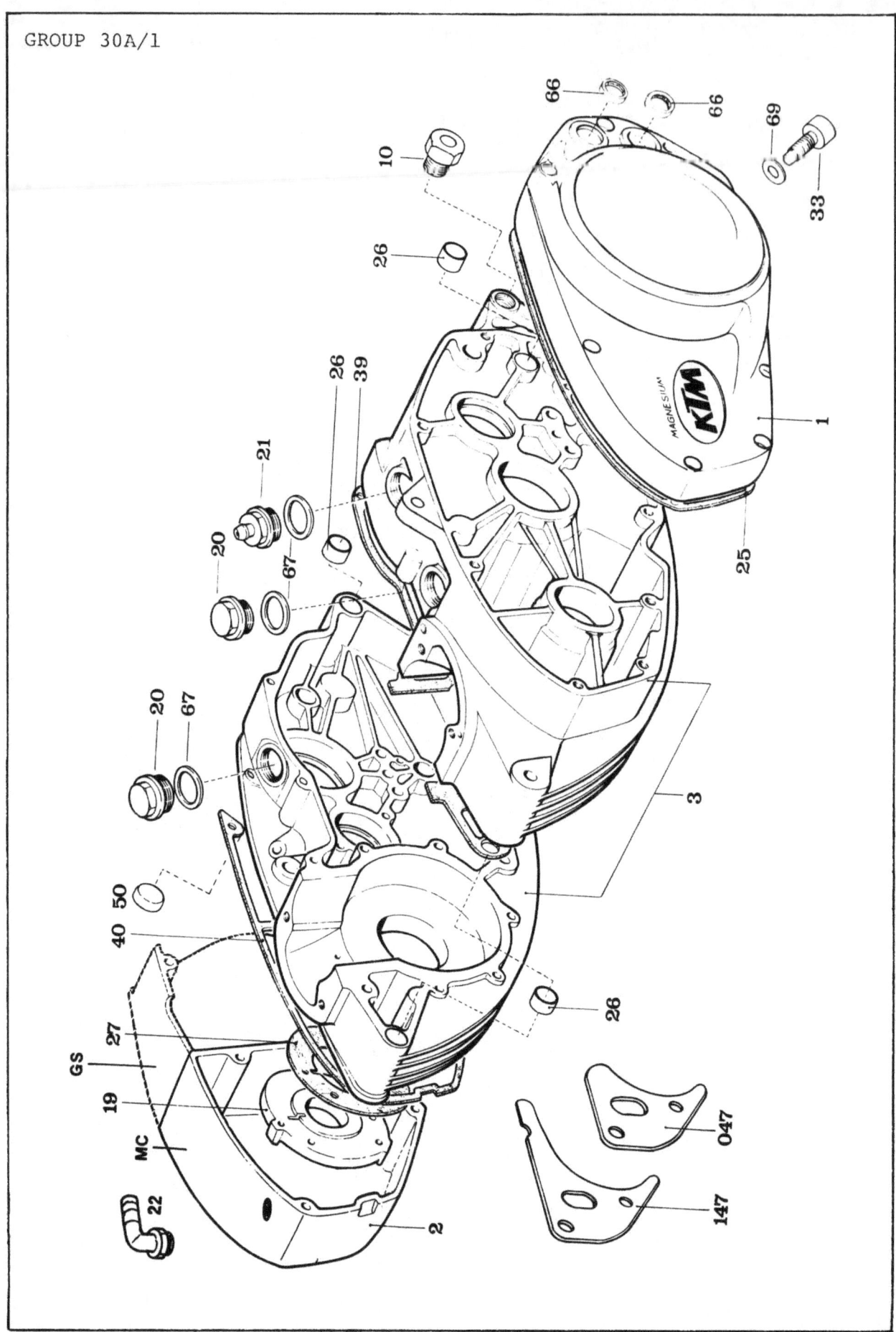

GROUP 30A/1   CRANKCASE I

PICTURE	PART NO.	DESCRIPTION	125	175	250	400
1	51.30.001.510	Clutch cover (for 14mm kickstarter shaft)	1	1	-	-
-	54.30.001.510	Clutch cover (for 17mm kickstarter shaft)	-	-	1	1
2	55.30.002.110	Ignition case cover (for crank case 55.30.001.110) GS	-	-	-	1
-	51.30.002.110	Ignition case cover GS	1	1	1	1
-	55.30.102.110	Ignition case cover MC	-	-	-	1
-	51.30.102.010	Ignition case cover MC	1	1	1	-
3	51.30.000.010	Engine case cpl.	1	-	-	-
-	52.30.000.010	Engine case cpl.	-	1	-	-
-	54.30.000.110	Engine case cpl.	-	-	1	-
-	55.30.000.110	Engine case cpl. for crankshaft 55.30.018.101	-	-	-	1
-	55.30.000.010	Engine case cpl. for crankshaft 55.30.018.001	-	-	-	NB
10	55.30.010.000	Engine mount bushing 3mm	NB	NB	NB	NB
10	52.30.010.100	Engine mount bushing	1	1	1	1
19	51.30.019.500	Seal retaining plate R/S	1	1	-	-
-	54.30.019.000	Seal retaining plate R/S	-	-	1	-
-	55.30.019.000	Seal retaining plate R/S	-	-	-	1
20	51.30.020.000	Screw plug	2	2	2	2
21	51.30.021.000	Breather plug	1	1	1	1
22	51.30.022.000	Elbow Screw nipple (breather kit)	1	1	1	1
25	51.30.025.000	Clutch case gasket	1	1	1	1
26	51.30.026.100	Dowel 17mm	3	3	3	3
27	51.30.027.000	Flange gasket R/S	1	1	-	-
-	54.30.027.000	Flange gasket R/S	-	-	1	1
33	54.33.033.100	Adjusting bolt	-	-	1	1
-	51.33.033.000	Adjusting bolt	1	1	-	-

GROUP 30A/1

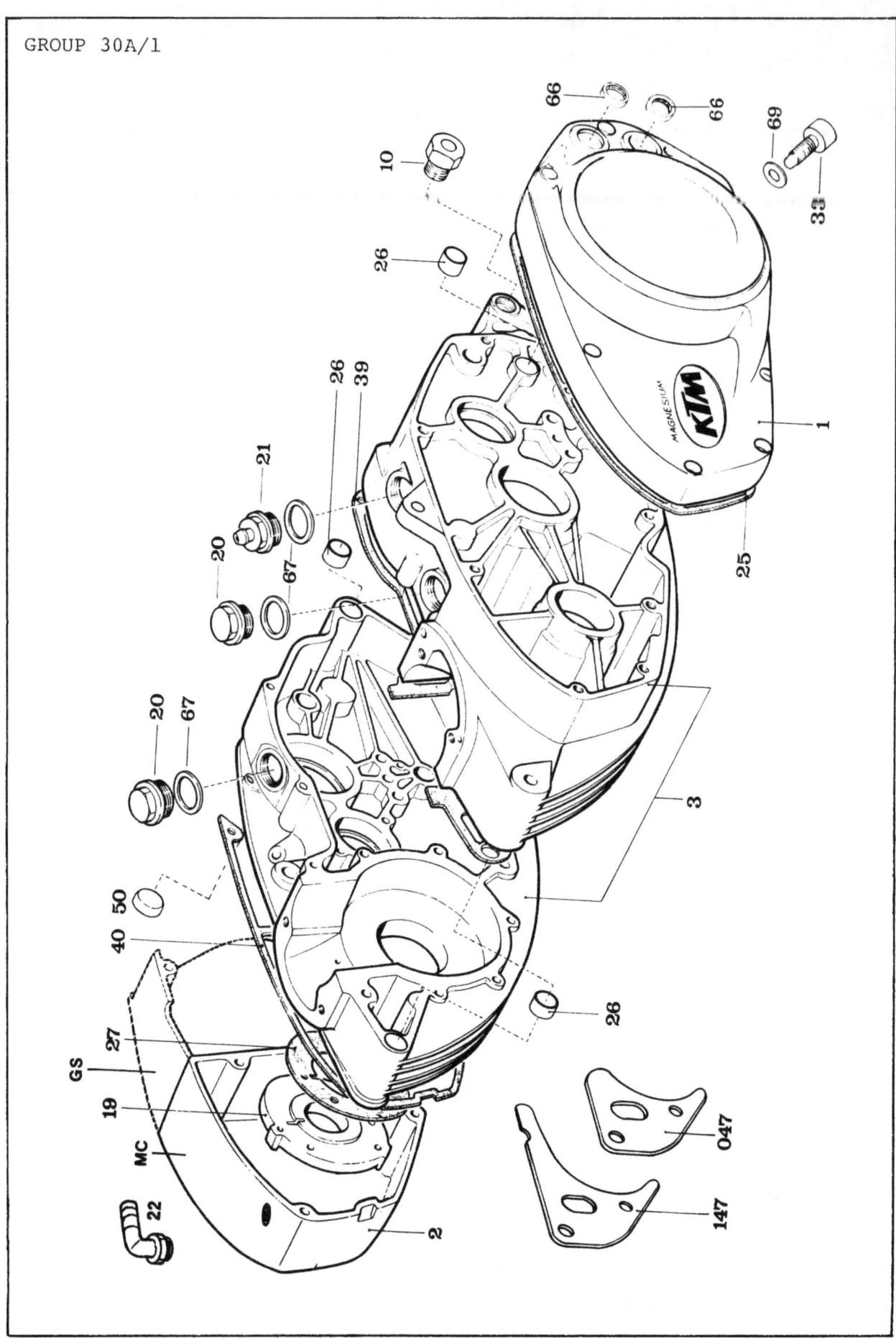

GROUP 30A/1 - CRANKCASE I

PICTURE	PART NO.	DESCRIPTION	125	175	250	400
39	54.30.039.000	Engine case gasket	1	1	1	1
40	51.30.040.000	Ignition case gasket	1	1	1	1
147	51.30.047.200	Crank case protector 14T MC	NB	NB	NB	NB
-	51.30.047.400	Crank case protector 13T MC	NB	NB	NB	NB
047	51.30.047.300	Crank case protector 14T GS	NB	NB	NB	NB
-	51.30.047.500	Crank case protector 13T GS	NB	NB	NB	NB
-	51.30.047.600	Crank case protector 12T MC & GS	NB	NB	NB	NB
50	51.30.057.000	Sheet metal plug for shifting shaft	1	1	1	1
66	0760 142240	Radial seal ring BA 14x22x4 DIN 3760	2	2	1	1
67	0603 263015	Seal ring 26x30.1.5 DIN 7603	3	3	3	3
69	0603 122201	Seal ring 12.2x20x1 DIN 7603	1	1	1	1
-	51.30.100.000	Gasket set for 125cc engine	1	-	-	-
-	52.30.100.000	Gasket set for 175cc engine	-	1	-	-
-	54.30.100.000	Gasket set for 250cc engine	-	-	1	-
-	55.30.100.000	Gasket set for 400cc engine	-	-	-	1

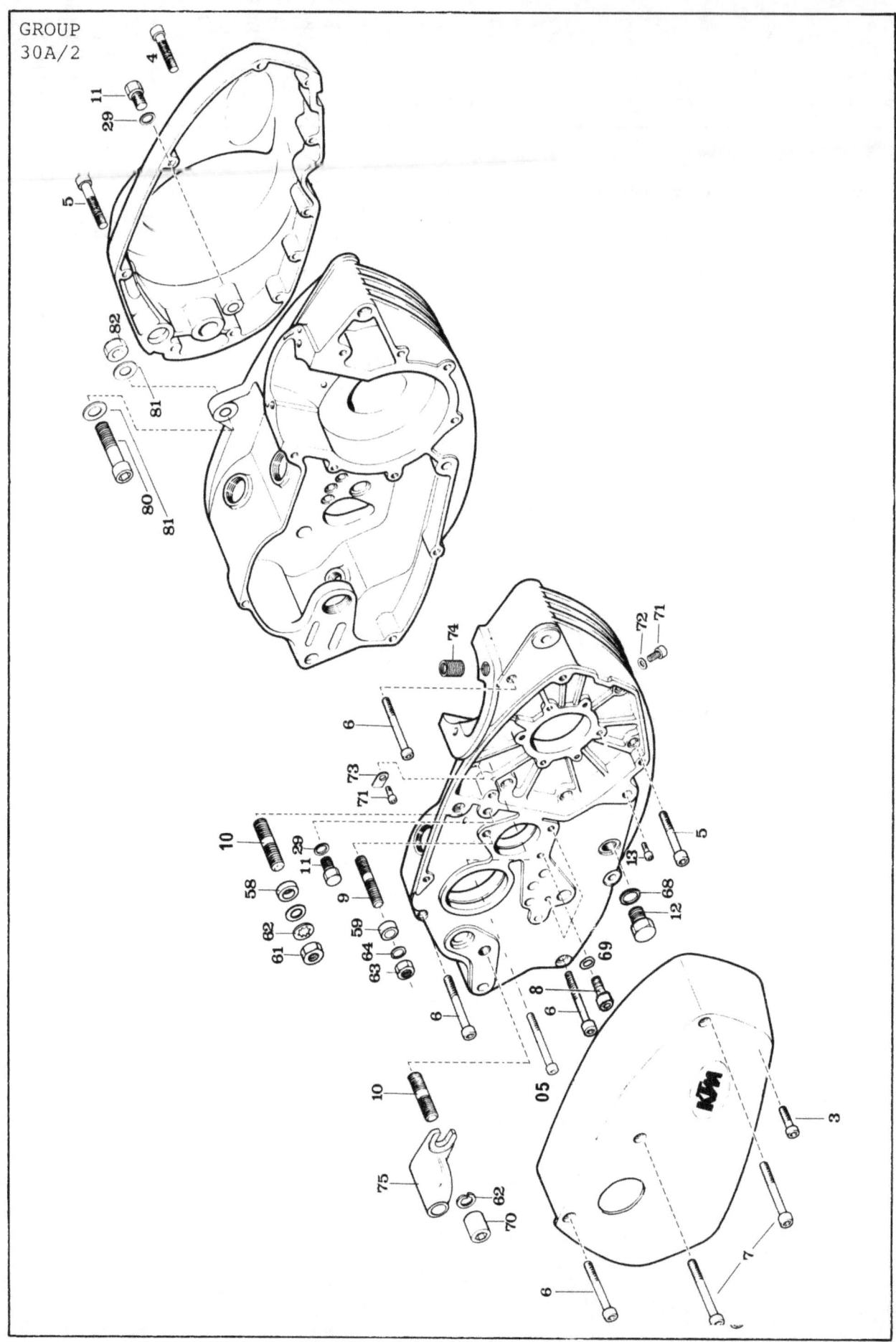

GROUP 30A/2 - CRANKCASE II

PICTURE	PART NO.	DESCRIPTION	125	175	250	400
3	0912 060203	Allen head screw M 6x20/8G DIN 912	1	1	1	1
4	0912 060353	Allen head screw M 6x35/8G DIN 912	9	9	9	9
5	0912 060553	Allen head screw M 6x55/8G DIN 912	7	7	6	1
05	0912 060603	Allen head screw M 6x60/8G DIN 912	-	-	1	5
6	0912 060653	Allen head screw M 6x65/8G DIN 912	7	7	7	8
7	0912 060753	Allen head screw M 6x75/8G DIN 912	2	2	2	-
8	0912 060162	Allen head screw M 6x16 DIN 912	3	3	3	3
9	0940 080302	Stud M 8x30 DIN 940	1	1	1	1
10	51.30.056.000	Stud M 10x45 DIN 835	2	2	2	2
11	0604 081153	Plug AM 8x1x15/8G DIN 7604	2	2	2	2
12	0604 121503	Plug AM 12x1.5/8G DIN 7604	1	1	1	1
13	0912 050163	Allen head screw M 5x16/8G DIN 912	6	6	6	-
-	0912 050143	Allen head screw M 5x14/8G DIN 912	-	-	-	6
29	0603 081210	Seal ring 8.2x12x1 DIN 7603	2	2	2	2
58	51.30.058.100	Washer for crank case protector 20mm, 6mm	NB	NB	NB	NB
59	51.30.059.000	Washer for crank case protector 15mm, 7.5mm	NB	NB	NB	NB
61	0934 100003	Hexagon nut M 10 DIN 934	1	1	1	1
62	0137 100000	Spring washer B 10 DIN 137	3	3	3	3
63	0934 080003	Hexagon nut M 8 DIN 934	1	1	1	1
64	0137 080000	Spring washer M 8 DIN 137	1	1	1	1
68	0603 122171	Seal ring 12.2x17x1 DIN 7603	1	1	1	1
69	0137 060000	Spring washer B 6 DIN 137	3	3	3	3

GROUP
30A/2

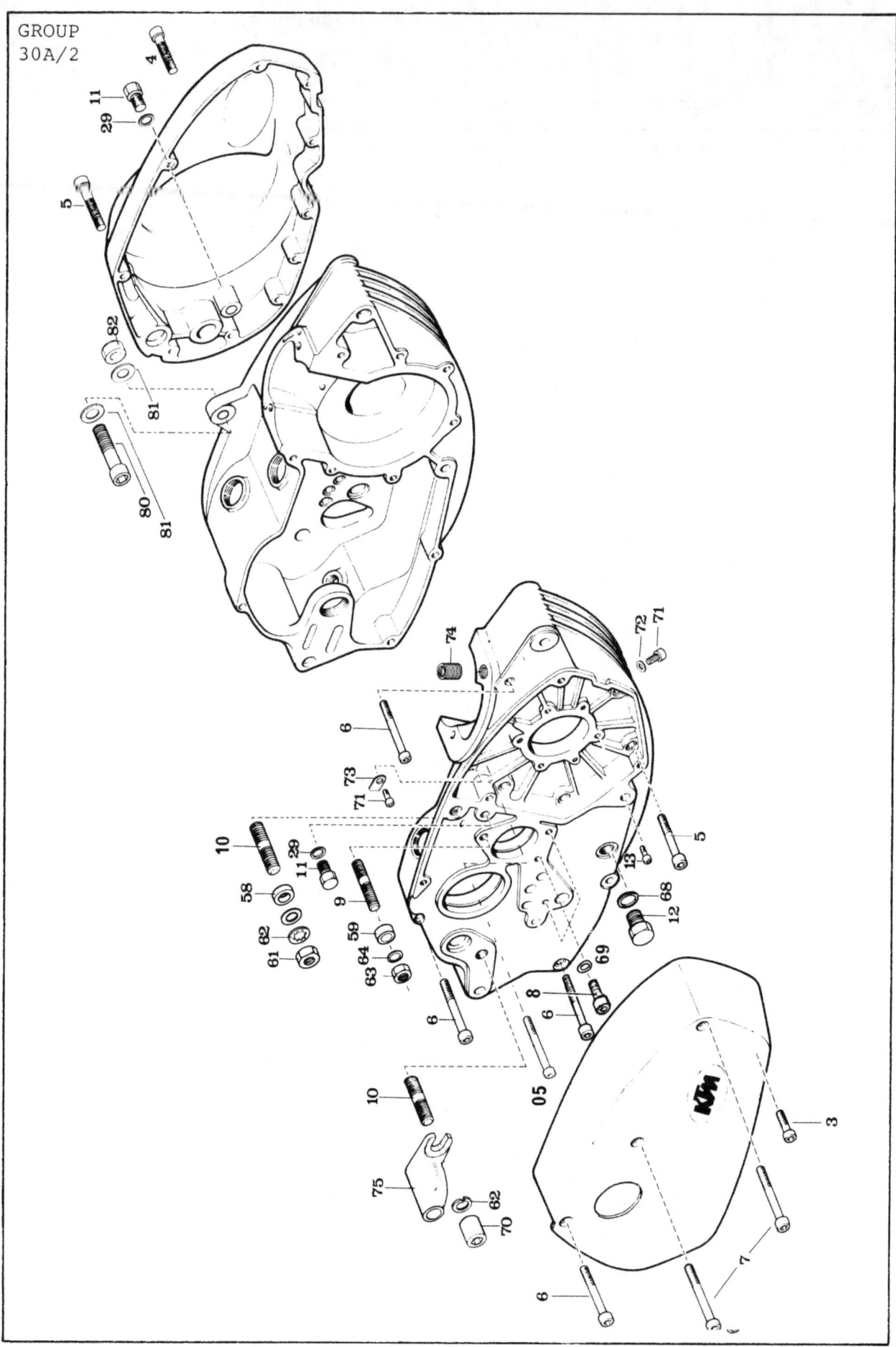

8

GROUP 30A/2 - CRANKCASE II

PICTURE	PART NO.	DESCRIPTION	125	175	250	400
70	51.30.148.000	Inside hexagon nut M 10	1	1	1	1
71	0912 050083	Allen head screw M 5x8 DIN 912	2	2	2	2
72	0603 051015	Seal ring 5x10x1.5 DIN 7603	1	1	1	1
73	51.30.049.000	Retaining plate	1	1	1	1
74	51.30.054.000	Threaded bushing	1	1	1	1
75	52.03.052.400	Spacer	1	1	1	1
80	0912 100403	Allen head screw M 10x40	1	1	1	1
81	0125 100000	Washer 10.5 DIN 125	2	2	2	2
82	0985 100003	Self locking nut M 10 DIN 985	1	1	1	1

GROUP 30/B

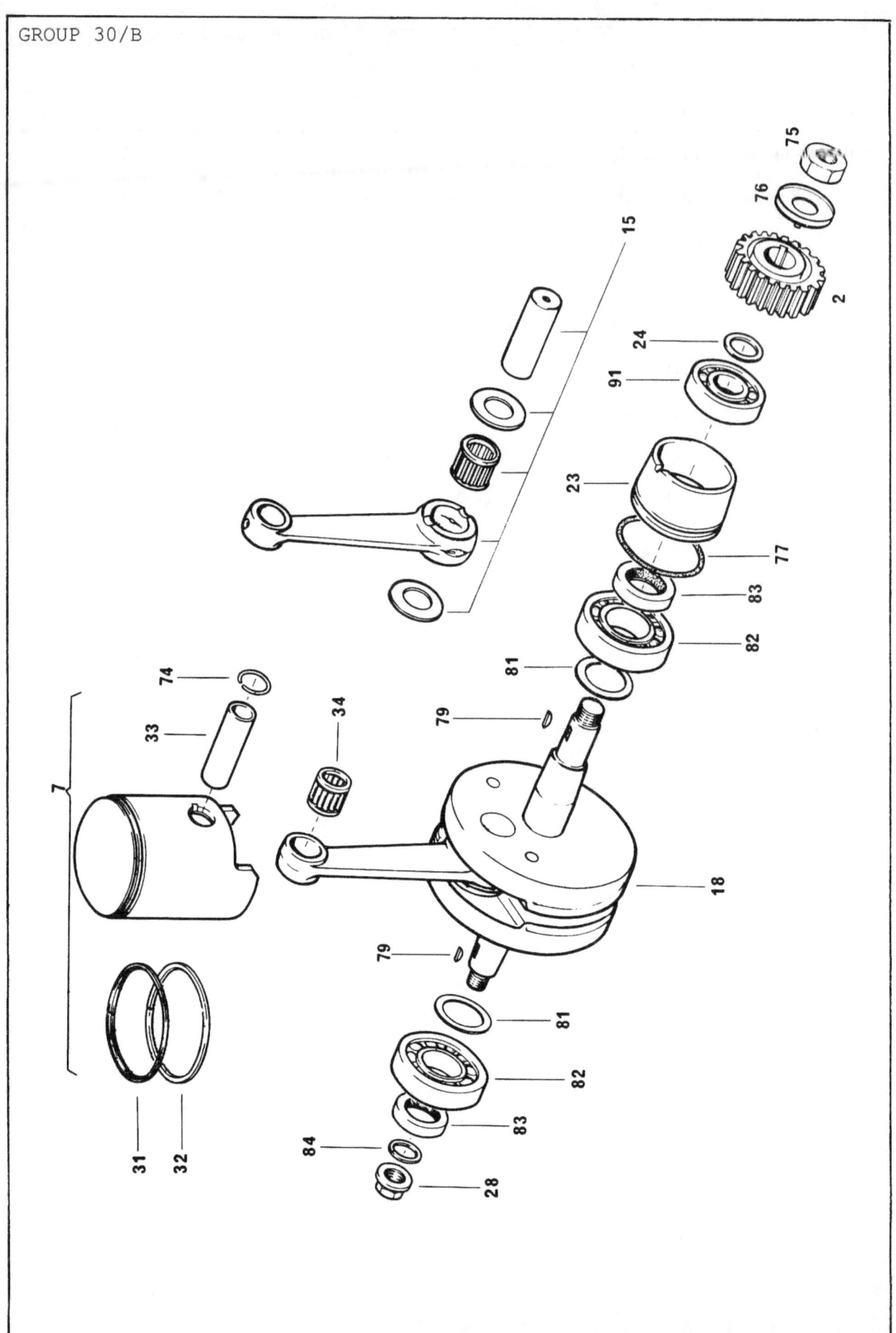

GROUP 30/B - CRANKSHAFT, PISTON 125/175

PICTURE	PART NO.	DESCRIPTION	125	175
2		Pinion, only available together with outer clutch hub		
7	50.30.007.000	Piston 54mm cpl.	1	-
-	50.30.007.100	Piston 54.25mm cpl.	NB	-
-	50.30.007.200	Piston 54.50mm cpl.	NB	-
-	50.30.007.300	Piston 54.75mm cpl.	NB	-
-	50.30.007.400	Piston 55mm cpl.	NB	-
7	52.30.007.500	Piston 63.5mm cpl.	-	1
-	52.30.007.600	Piston 63.75mm cpl.	-	NB
-	52.20.007.700	Piston 64mm cpl.	-	NB
-	52.30.007.800	Piston 64.5mm cpl.	-	NB
15	51.30.015.044	Connecting rod repair kit	NB	NB
18	51.30.018.700	Crankshaft	1	-
-	52.30.018.000	Crankshaft	-	1
23	51.30.023.600	Spacer	1	1
24	51.30.024.000	Spacer	1	1
28	51.30.028.100	Magneto nut M 12x1 L/S	1	1
31	50.30.031.000	L-ring 54mm	1	-
-	50.30.031.100	L-ring 54.25mm	NB	-
-	50.30.031.200	L-ring 54.50mm	NB	-
-	50.30.031.300	L-ring 54.75mm	NB	-
31	52.30.031.500	L-ring 63.5mm	-	1
-	52.30.031.600	L-ring 63.75mm	-	NB
-	52.30.031.700	L-ring 64.00mm	-	NB
-	52.30.031.800	L-ring 64.50mm	-	NB
32	50.30.032.000	Square ring 54mm	1	-
-	50.30.032.100	Square ring 54.25mm	NB	-

GROUP 30/B

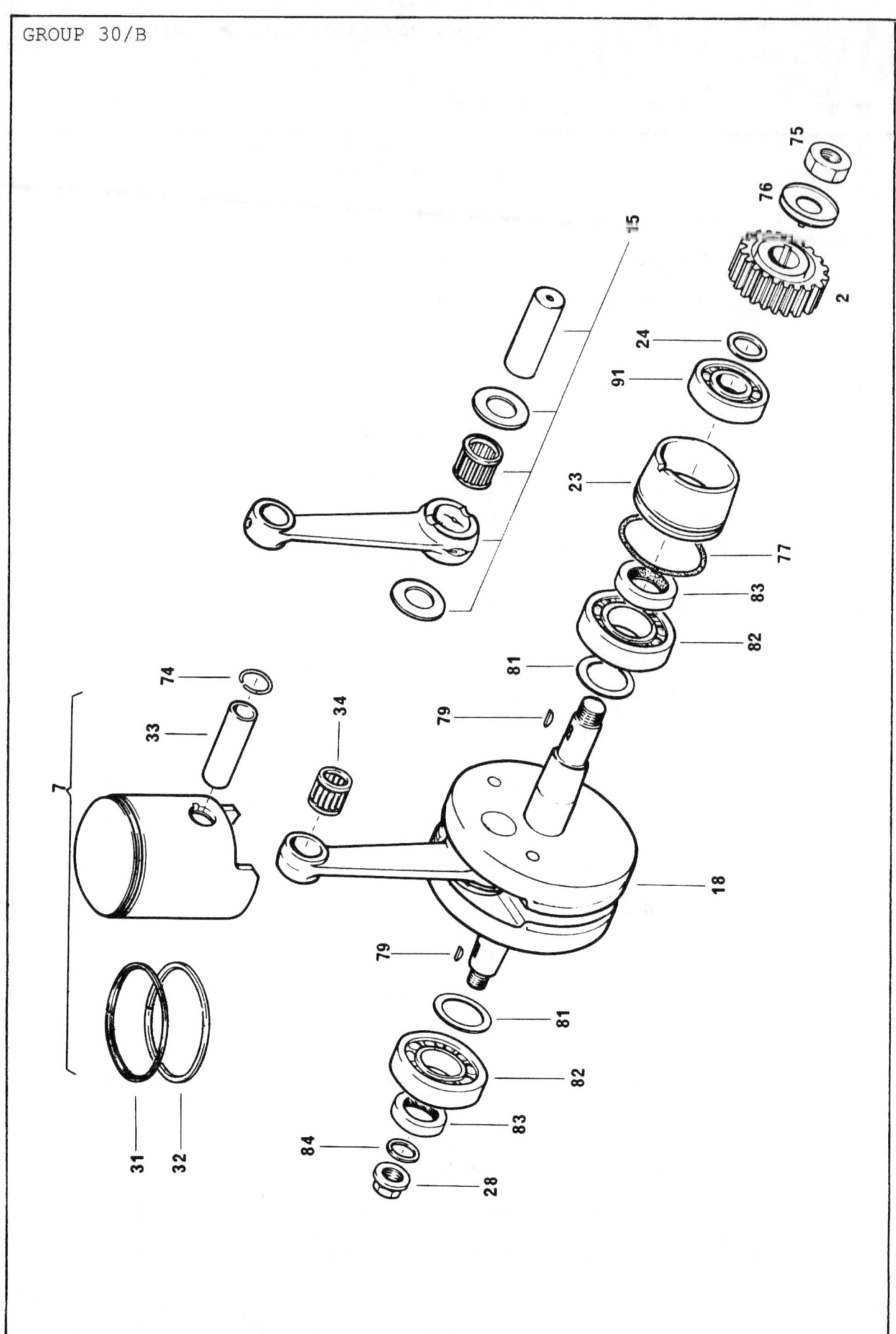

GROUP 30/B - CRANKSHAFT, PISTON 125/175

PICTURE	PART NO.	DESCRIPTION	125	175
-	50.30.032.200	Square ring 54.5mm	NB	-
-	50.30.032.300	Square ring 54.75mm	NB	-
32	52.30.032.000	Square ring 63.5mm	-	1
-	52.30.032.200	Square ring 63.75mm	-	NB
-	52.30.032.300	Square ring 64.00mm	-	NB
-	52.30.032.400	Square ring 64.45mm	-	NB
33	52.30.033.100	Wrist pin 15x56.4	-	1
-	51.30.033.000	Wrist pin 15x46.5	1	-
34	51.30.034.000	Needle bearing 14x19x20	1	1
74	52.30.074.000	Retaining clip C 14 DIN 73 123	2	2
75	0936 140503	Hexagon head nut M 14x1.5 DIN 936	1	1
76	51.30.048.500	Flat washer	1	-
-	52.30.048.000	Flat washer	-	1
77	0770 222400	O-ring 2-224	1	1
79	0888 030050	Woodruff key 3x5 DIN 6888	2	2
81	54.30.081.100	Shim washer 25x35.0.1	NB	NB
-	54.30.081.200	Shim washer 25x35x0.15	NB	NB
-	54.30.081.300	Shim washer 25x35x0.3	NB	NB
82	52.30.082.200	Shoulder bearing L 25 DIN 615	2	2
83	0760 253570	Radial seal ring 25x35x7	2	2
84	0137 120000	Spring washer B 12 DIN 137	1	1
91	0625 063020	Ball bearing 6302 C3 SV 41,DIN 625	1	1

GROUP 30/B

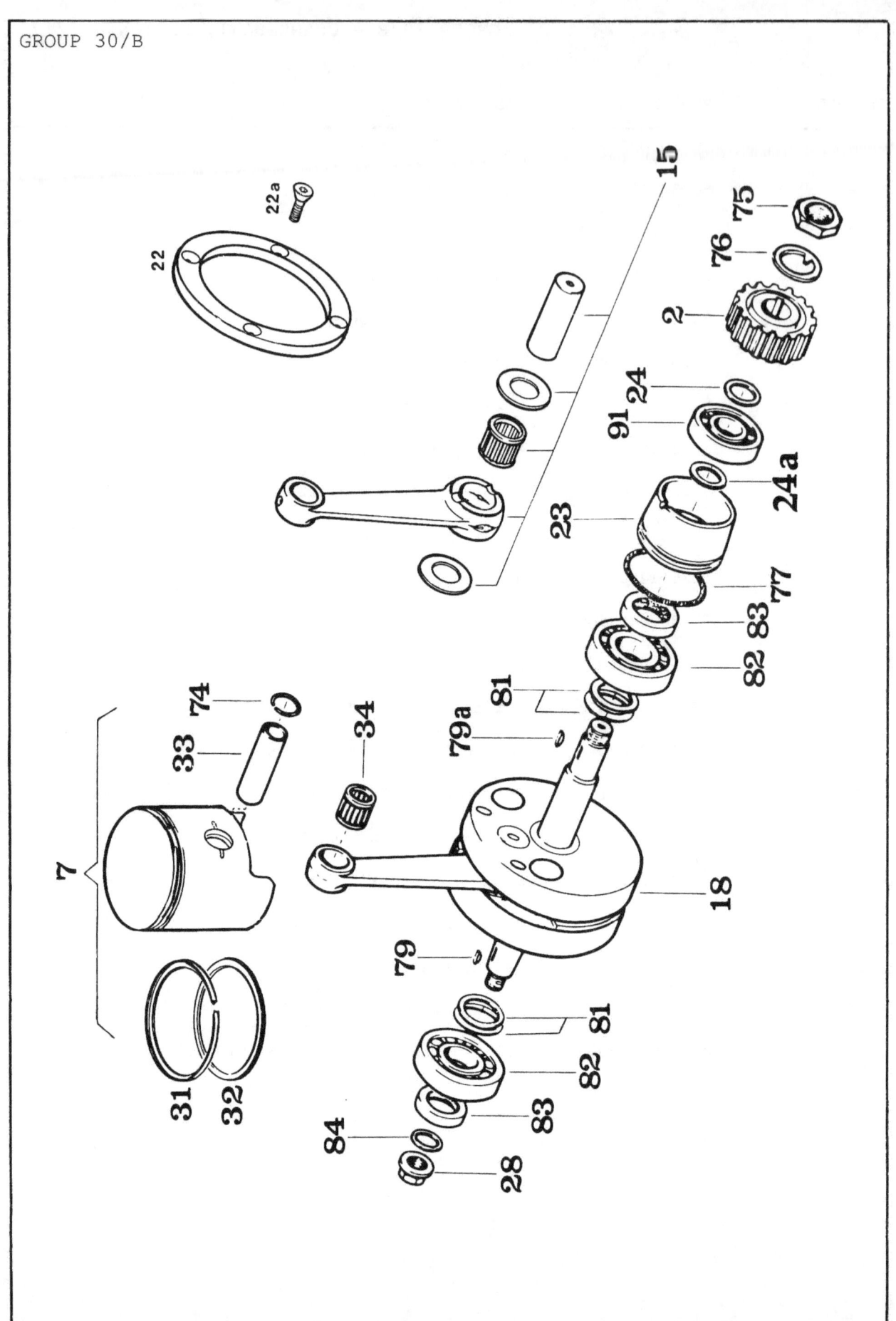

GROUP 30/B - CRANKSHAFT, PISTON 250/400

PICTURE	PART NO.	DESCRIPTION	250	400
2		Pinion 25-T only available together with outer clutch hub		
7	54.30.007.000	Piston 71.00mm cpl.	1	-
-	54.30.007.200	Piston 71.25mm cpl.	NB	-
-	54.30.007.300	Piston 71.50mm cpl.	NB	-
-	54.30.007.400	Piston 72.00mm cpl.	NB	-
-	55.30.007.400	Piston 81.00mm cpl.	-	NB
-	55.30.007.500	Piston 81.25mm cpl.	-	NB
-	55.30.007.600	Piston 81.50mm cpl.	-	NB
-	55.30.007.700	Piston 81.75mm cpl.	-	NB
15	54.30.015.044	Connecting rod repair kit	1	-
-	55.30.015.044	Connecting rod repair kit	-	1
18	54.30.018.300	Crankshaft assy.	1	-
-	55.30.018.101	Crankshaft cpl. w/flyrings	-	NB
-	55.30.018.001	Crankshaft cpl. wo/flyrings	-	1
22	55.30.022.000	Flyring	-	2
22A	0991 060122	Allen flat head screw M 6x12 DIN 7991	-	8
23	54.30.023.300	Spacer	1	-
-	55.30.023.000	Spacer	-	1
24	54.30.024.000	Spacer	1	1
24A	54.30.124.000	Spacer	1	1
28	51.30.028.100	Magneto nut M 12x1 L/S	1	1
31	54.30.031.000	L-ring 71.00mm x 2	1	-
-	54.30.031.200	L-ring 71.25mm x 2	NB	-
-	54.30.031.300	L-ring 71.50mm x 2	NB	-
-	54.30.031.400	L-ring 72.00mm x 2	NB	-
-	55.30.031.400	L-ring 81.00mm x 2	-	1

GROUP 30/B

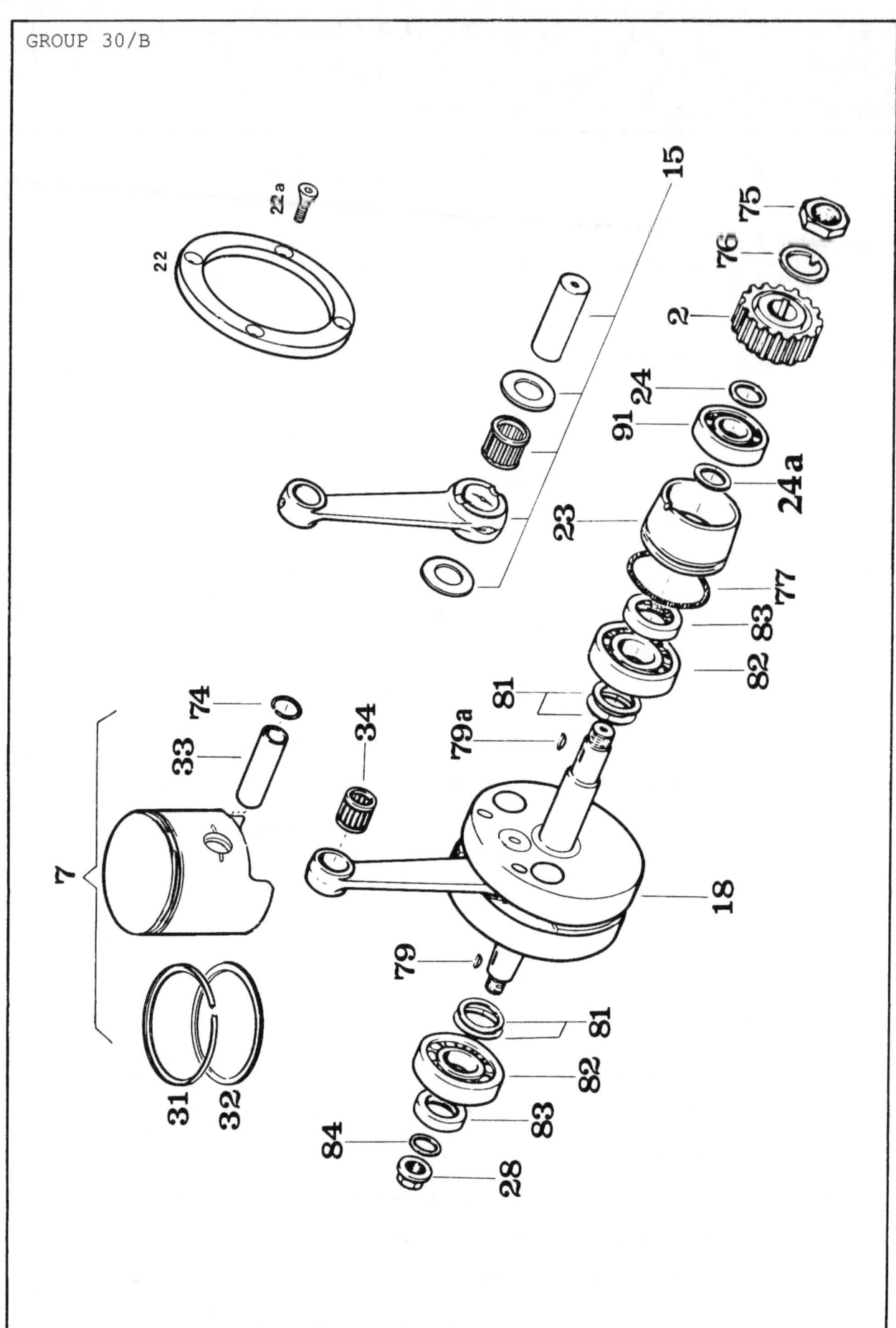

16

GROUP 30/B - CRANKSHAFT, PISTON 250/400

PICTURE	PART NO.	DESCRIPTION	250	400
-	55.30.031.500	L-ring 81.25mm x 2	-	NB
-	55.30.031.600	L-ring 81.50mm x 2	-	NB
-	55.30.031.700	L-ring 81.75mm x 2	-	NB
32	54.30.032.000	Square ring 71.00 x 2	1	-
-	54.30.032.200	Square ring 71.25 x 2	NB	-
-	54.30.032.300	Square ring 71.50 x 2	NB	-
-	54.30.032.400	Square ring 72.00 x 2	NB	-
-	55.30.032.400	Square ring 81.00 x 2	-	1
-	55.30.032.500	Square ring 81.25 x 2	-	NB
-	55.30.032.600	Square ring 81.50 x 2	-	NB
-	55.30.032.700	Square ring 81.75 x 2	-	NB
33	54.30.033.000	Wrist pin 18x60.3	1	-
-	55.30.033.000	Wrist pin	-	1
34	54.30.034.000	Needle bearing 18x22x25	1	1
74	54.30.074.000	Retaining clip C 18 DIN 73123	2	2
75	0936 181503	Hexagon head screw M 18x1.5 DIN 936	1	1
76	54.30.048.000	Flat washer 22mm	1	1
77	0770 222700	O-ring 2-227	1	-
-	0770 213900	O-ring 2-139	-	1
79	0888 030050	Woodruff key 3x5 DIN 688	1	1
79A	0888 040050	Woodruff key 4x5 DIN 6888	1	1
81	54.30.081.100	Shim washer 25x35x.1	NB	NB
-	54.30.081.200	Shim washer 25x35x.15	NB	NB
-	54.30.081.300	Shim washer 25x35x.3	NB	NB
82	54.30.082.000	Shoulder bearing M 25 DIN 615	2	2
83	0760 253570	Radial seal ring 25x35x7	2	2
84	0137 120000	Spring washer B 12 DIN 137	1	1
91	0625 062040	Ball bearing 6204 C3 SV 41 DIN 625	1	1

GROUP 30/C
125

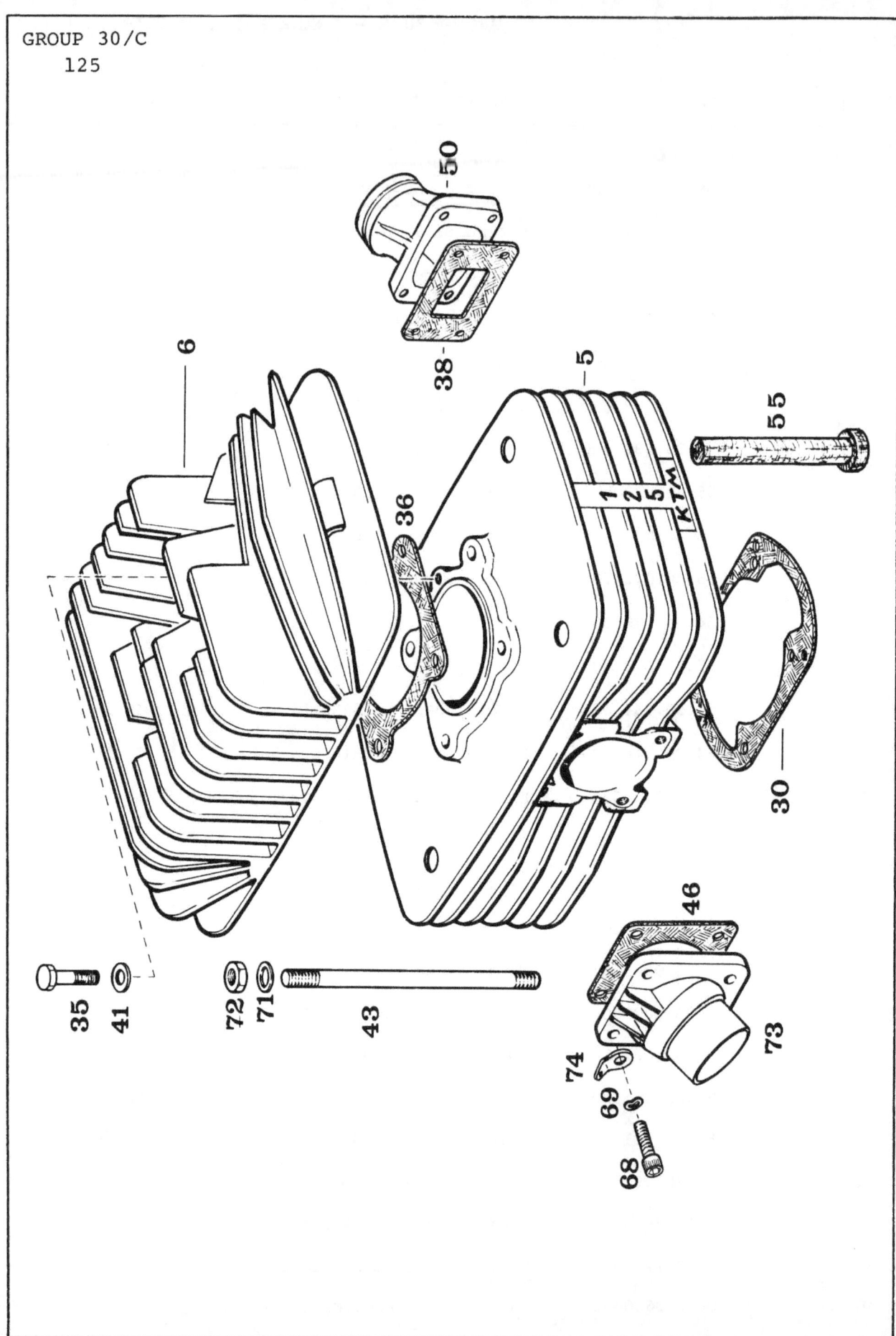

GROUP 30/C - CYLINDER 125

PICTURE	PART NO.	DESCRIPTION	125
5	51.30.005.000	Cylinder	1
-	51.30.005.050	Cylinder liner	NB
6	51.30.006.000	Cylinder head	1
30	51.30.030.000	Cylinder base gasket 0.2mm	NB
-	51.30.030.100	Cylinder base gasket 0.3mm	NB
-	51.30.030.200	Cylinder base gasket 0.5mm	NB
-	51.30.030.300	Cylinder base gasket 0.75mm	NB
35	0931 080402	Hexagon head screw M 8x40 DIN 931	1
36	51.30.036.000	Cylinder head gasket	1
38	51.30.038.000	Intake adapter gasket	1
41	0125 080000	Flat washer 8.4 DIN 125	1
43	51.30.043.100	Cylinder stud, 142mm long	4
46	51.30.046.000	Exhaust adapter gasket	1
50	51.30.050.600	Intake adapter manifold	1
55	54.30.055.000	Rubber	4
68	0912 060252	Allen head screw M 6x25	8
69	0137 060000	Spring washer B 6 DIN 137	8
71	0125 080000	Flat washer 8.4 DIN 125	4
72	0934 080003	Hexagon nut M 8 DIN 934	4
73	51.05.073.000	Exhaust flange	1
74	51.05.074.000	Retaining plate	2

GROUP 30/C
175

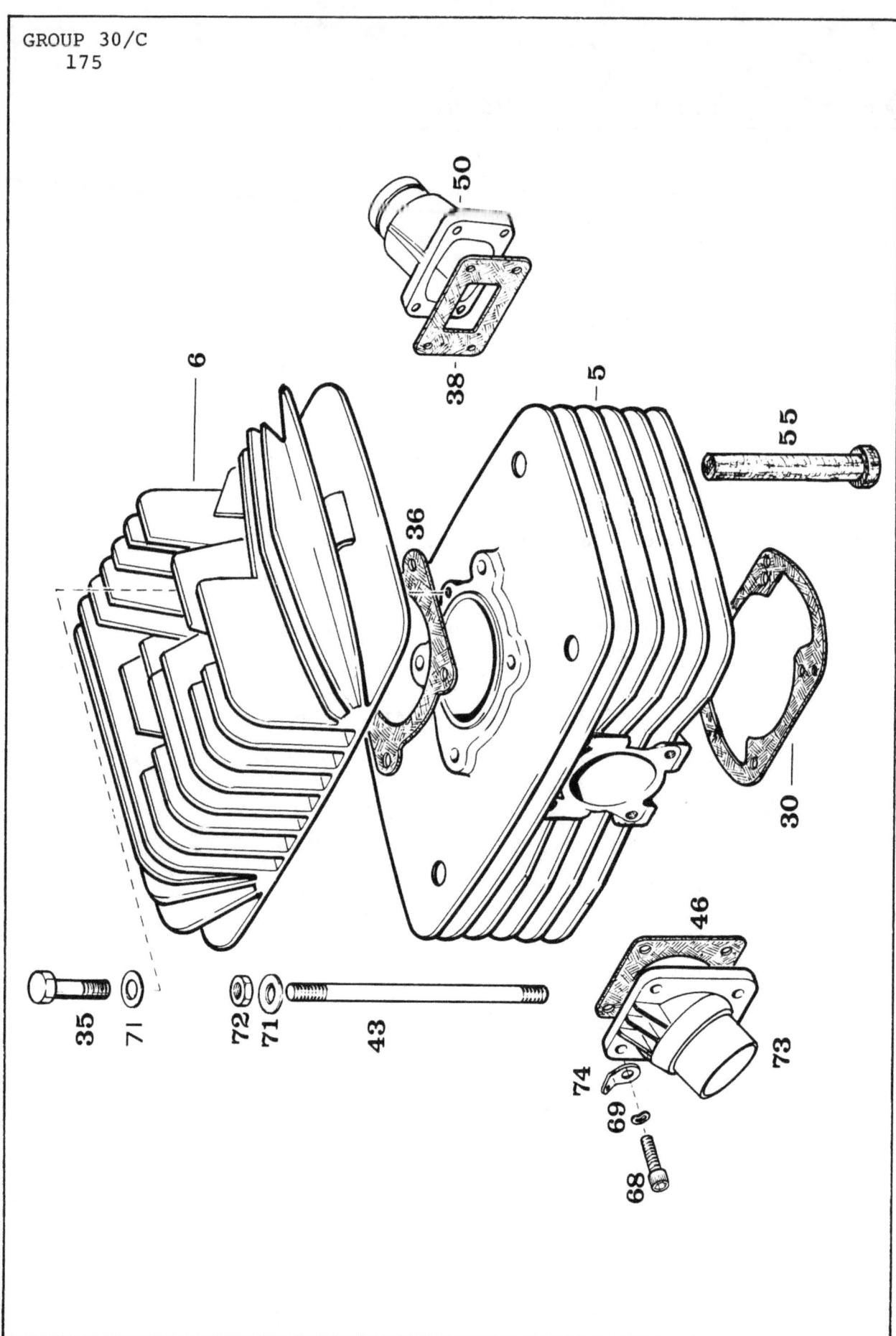

GROUP 30/C - CYLINDER 175

PICTURE	PART NO.	DESCRIPTION	175
5	52.30.005.500	Cylinder barrel 63.5	1
-	52.30.005.550	Cylinder liner	1
6	52.30.006.500	Cylinder head	1
30	52.30.030.500	Cylinder base gasket 0.2mm	NB
-	52.30.030.600	Cylinder base gasket 0.3mm	NB
-	52.30.030.700	Cylinder base gasket 0.5mm	NB
-	52.30.030.800	Cylinder base gasket 0.75mm	NB
-	52.30.030.900	Cylinder base gasket 1.0mm	NB
36	52.30.036.100	Cylinder head gasket 1.0mm	1
38	52.30.038.500	Induction manifold gasket	1
40	0931 080402	Hexagon head screw M 8x40 DIN 931	1
41	0125 080000	Flat washer 8.4 DIN 125	1
43	51.30.043.100	Cylinder stud M 8, 142mm long	4
46	52.30.046.500	Exhaust adapter gasket	1
50	52.30.050.500	Intake adapter	1
55	54.30.055.000	Rubber	4
68	0912 060252	Allen head screw M 6x25	8
69	0137 060000	Spring washer B 6, DIN 137	8
71	0125 080000	Flat washer 8.4 DIN 125	4
72	0934 080003	Hexagon nut M 8 DIN 934	4
73	52.05.073.500	Exhaust flange	1
74	51.05.074.000	Spring holder	2

GROUP 30/C
250/400

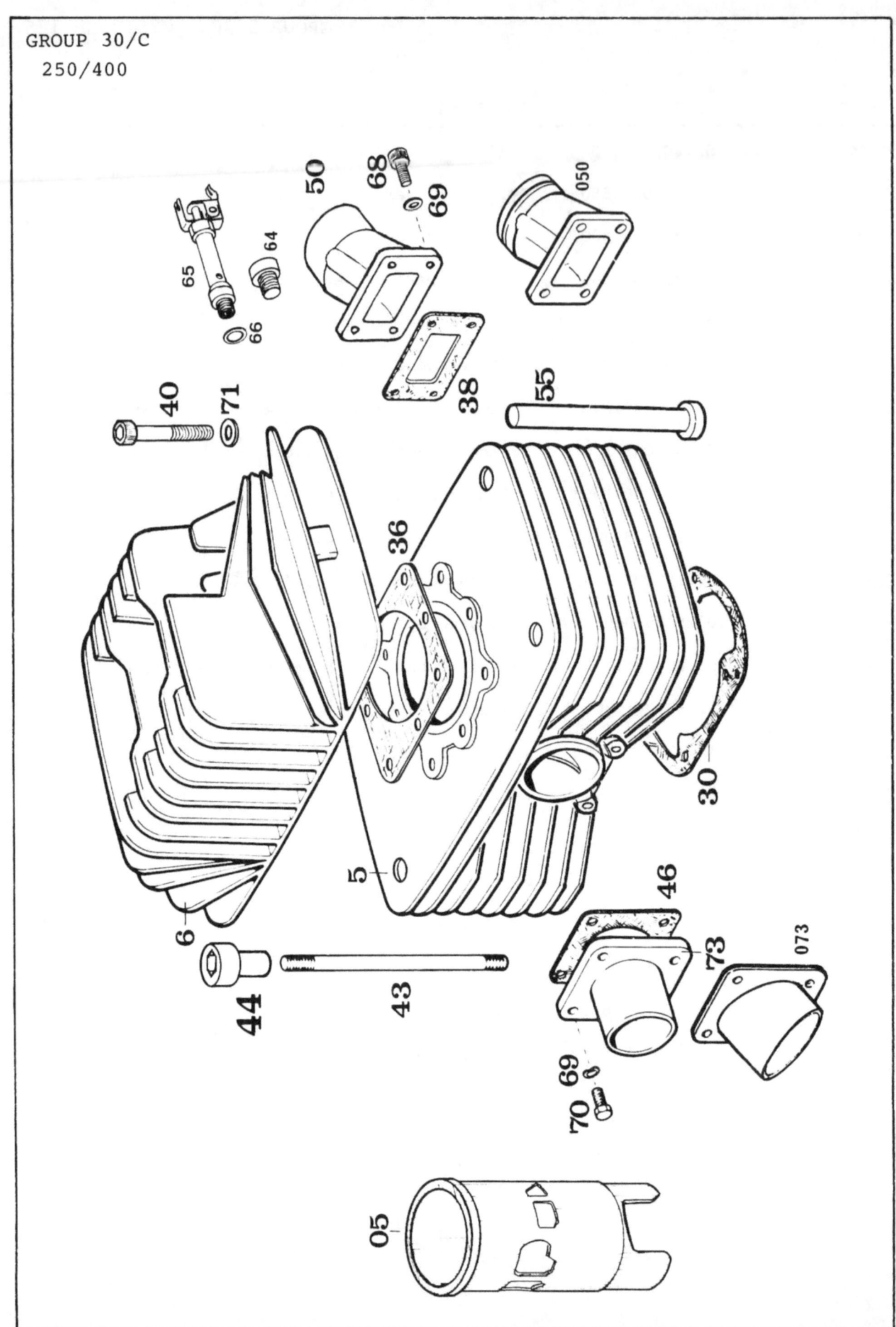

GROUP 30/C - CYLINDER 250/400

PICTURE	PART NO.	DESCRIPTION	250	400
5	54.30.005.500	Cylinder barrel 71mm	1	-
-	55.30.005.500	Cylinder barrel 81mm	-	1
05	54.30.005.550	Cylinder liner 71mm	1	-
-	55.30.005.550	Cylinder liner 81mm	-	1
6	54.30.006.100	Cylinder head GS	1	-
-	54.30.106.100	Cylinder head MC	1	-
-	55.30.006.300	Cylinder head GS	-	1
-	55.30.106.300	Cylinder head MC	-	1
30	54.30.030.000	Cylinder base gasket 0.2mm	NB	-
-	54.30.030.100	Cylinder base gasket 0.3mm	NB	-
-	54.30.030.200	Cylinder base gasket 0.5mm	NB	-
-	54.30.030.300	Cylinder base gasket 0.75mm	NB	-
-	54.30.030.400	Cylinder base gasket 1mm	NB	-
30	55.30.030.000	Cylinder base gasket 0.2mm	-	NB
-	55.30.030.100	Cylinder base gasket 0.3mm	-	NB
-	55.30.030.200	Cylinder base gasket 0.5mm	-	NB
-	55.30.030.300	Cylinder base gasket 0.75mm	-	NB
-	55.30.030.400	Cylinder base gasket 1mm	-	NB
36	54.30.036.100	Cylinder head gasket 1mm	1	-
-	55.30.036.000	Cylinder head gasket 1mm	-	1
38	54.30.038.000	Induction manifold gasket	1	-
-	55.30.038.000	Induction manifold gasket	-	1
40	0912 080452	Allen head screw M 8x45 DIN 912	4	4
43	51.30.043.000	Cylinder stud M8, 152mm long	4	4
44	55.30.044.000	Nut	4	4
46	52.30.046.000	Exhaust adapter gasket	1	1
50	54.30.050.400	Intake adapter GS	1	-

GROUP 30/C
250/400

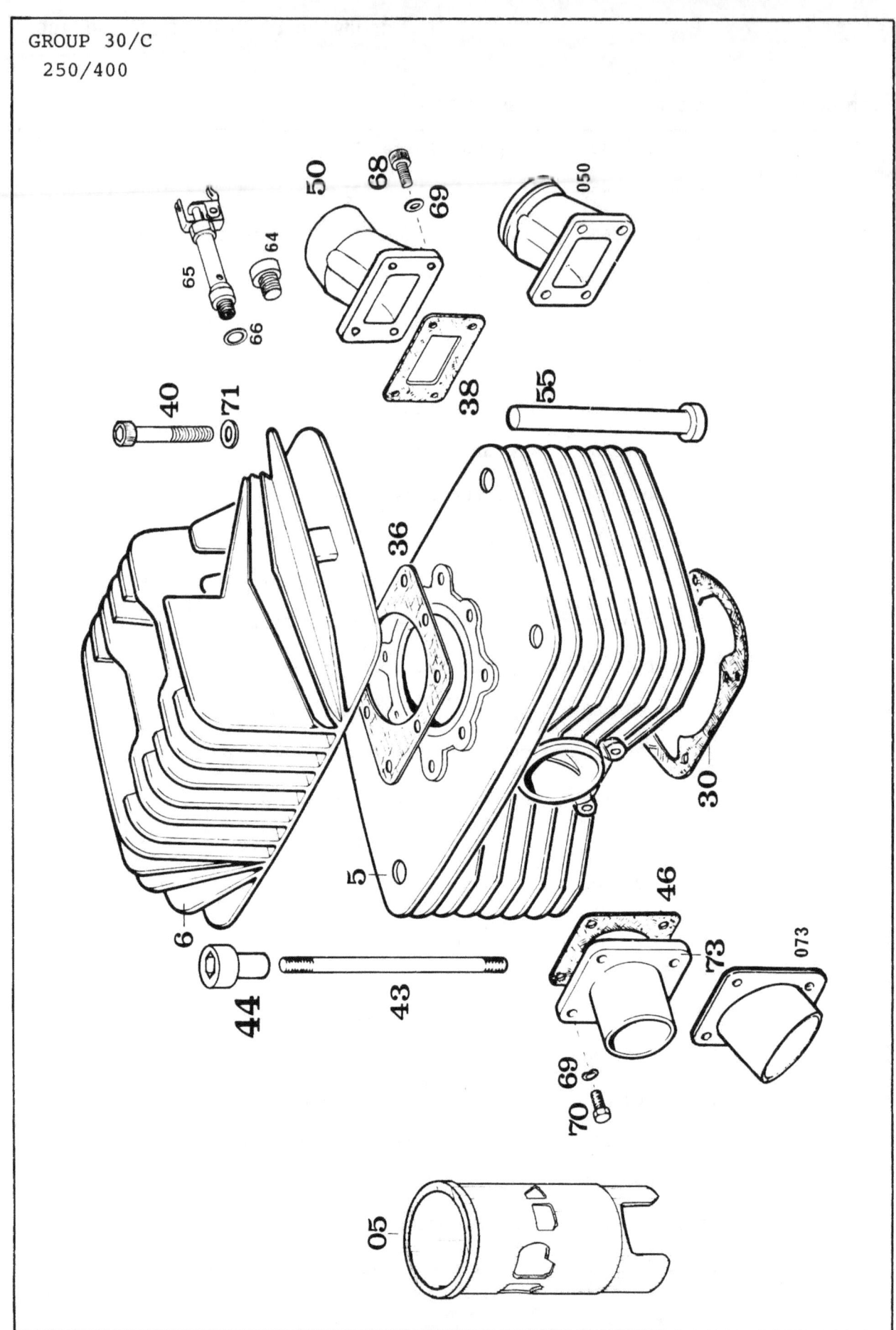

GROUP 30/C - CYLINDER 250/400

PICTURE	PART NO.	DESCRIPTION	250	400
-	54.30.150.400	Intake adapter MC	1	-
-	55.30.050.400	Intake adapter GS	-	1
-	55.30.150.400	Intake adapter MC	-	1
050	54.30.050.600	For use with rubber adapter GS & MC	1	-
55	54.30.055.000	Rubber	4	4
68	0912 060203	Allen head screw M 6x20 DIN 912	4	4
69	0137 060000	Spring washer B 6 DIN 137	8	8
70	0933 060163	Hexagon head screw M 6x16	4	4
71	0125 080000	Flat washer 8.4 DIN 125	4	4
73	54.05.073.000	Exhaust flange	-	1
64	55.30.064.000	Plug for decompressor hole	-	NB
65	55.30.065.000	Decompressor cpl.	-	1
66	55.30.066.000	Seal ring	-	1

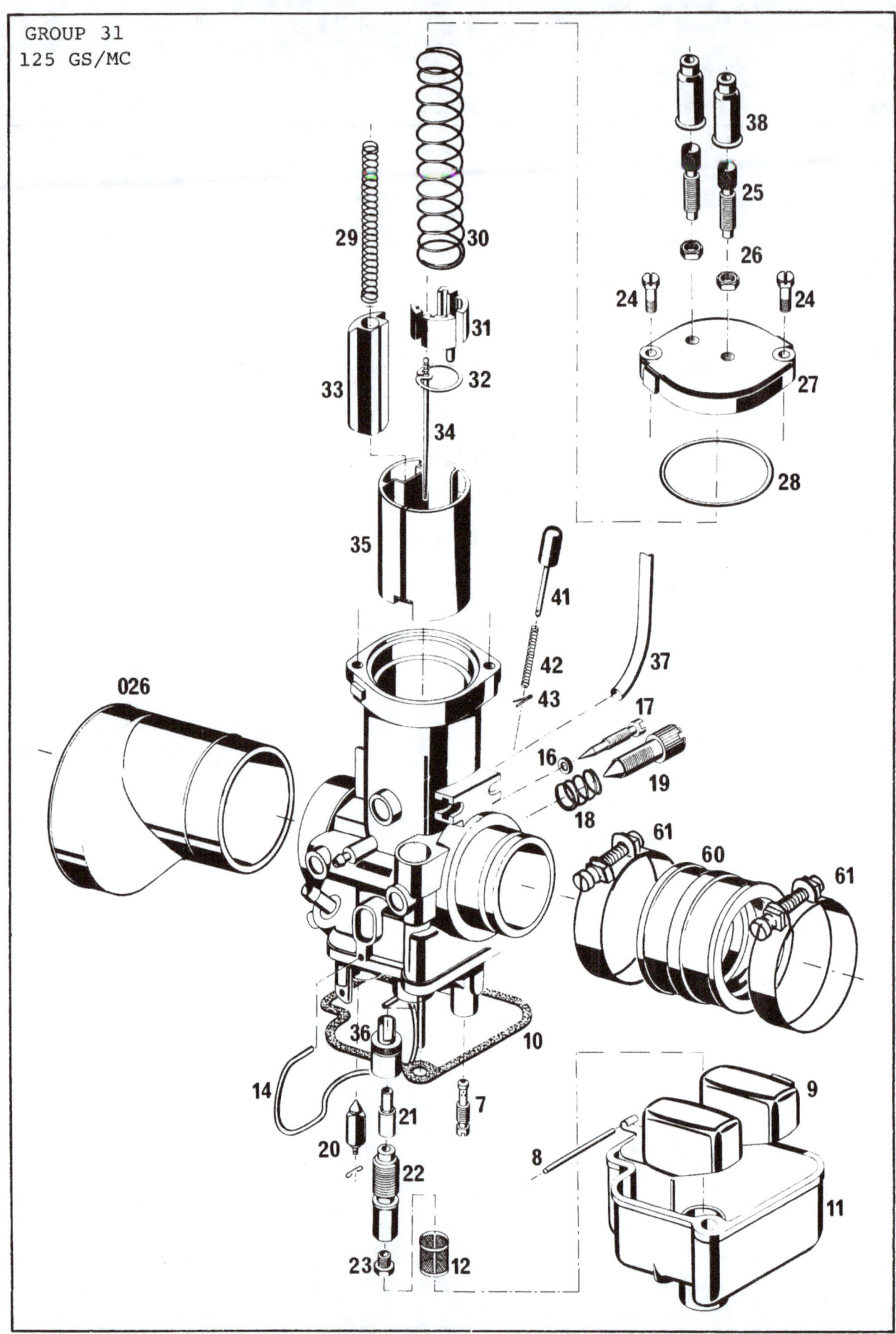

GROUP 31 - CARBURATOR 125 GS/MC

PICTURE	PART NO.	DESCRIPTION	BING NO.	GS	MC
-	51.31.101.144	Carburetor cpl.	54-34-104	1	-
-	51.31.101.244	Carburetor cpl.		-	1
7	52.31.107.000	Pilot jet, specify size	44-350	1	1
8	52.31.108.000	Spindle	52-058	1	1
9	52.31.109.000	Float	35-300	1	1
10	52.31.110.000	Seal	65-584	1	1
11	52.31.111.000	Float chamber body	30-569	1	1
12	51.31.112.000	Fuel filter	57-706	1	1
14	52.31.114.000	Float chamber clamp	61-479	1	1
16	51.31.116.100	O-ring	65-704	1	1
17	51.31.117.100	Pilot air adj. screw	50-039/101	1	1
18	52.31.118.000	Spring	60-322	1	1
19	52.31.119.000	Throttle stop adj. screw	50-072	1	1
20	51.31.120.100	Float needle	47-968	1	1
21	51.31.121.100	Needle jet, specify size	45-120	1	1
22	51.31.122.100	Jet holder	45-435	1	1
23	52.31.123.000	Jet, specify size	44-051	1	1
24	52.31.124.000	Top securing bolt	40-518	2	2
25	52.31.125.000	Cable adj.screw	50-050	2	1
26	52.31.126.000	Nut	42-605	2	1
27	51.31.127.100	Cover	20-672/101	1	-
-	51.31.127.200	Cover		-	1
28	54.31.128.000	Rubber seal ring	65-745	1	1
29	54.31.129.000	Spring	60-195	1	-
30	51.31.130.100	Spring	60-434	1	1
31	55.31.131.000	Spring retainer	26-512	1	1

GROUP 31
125 GS/MC

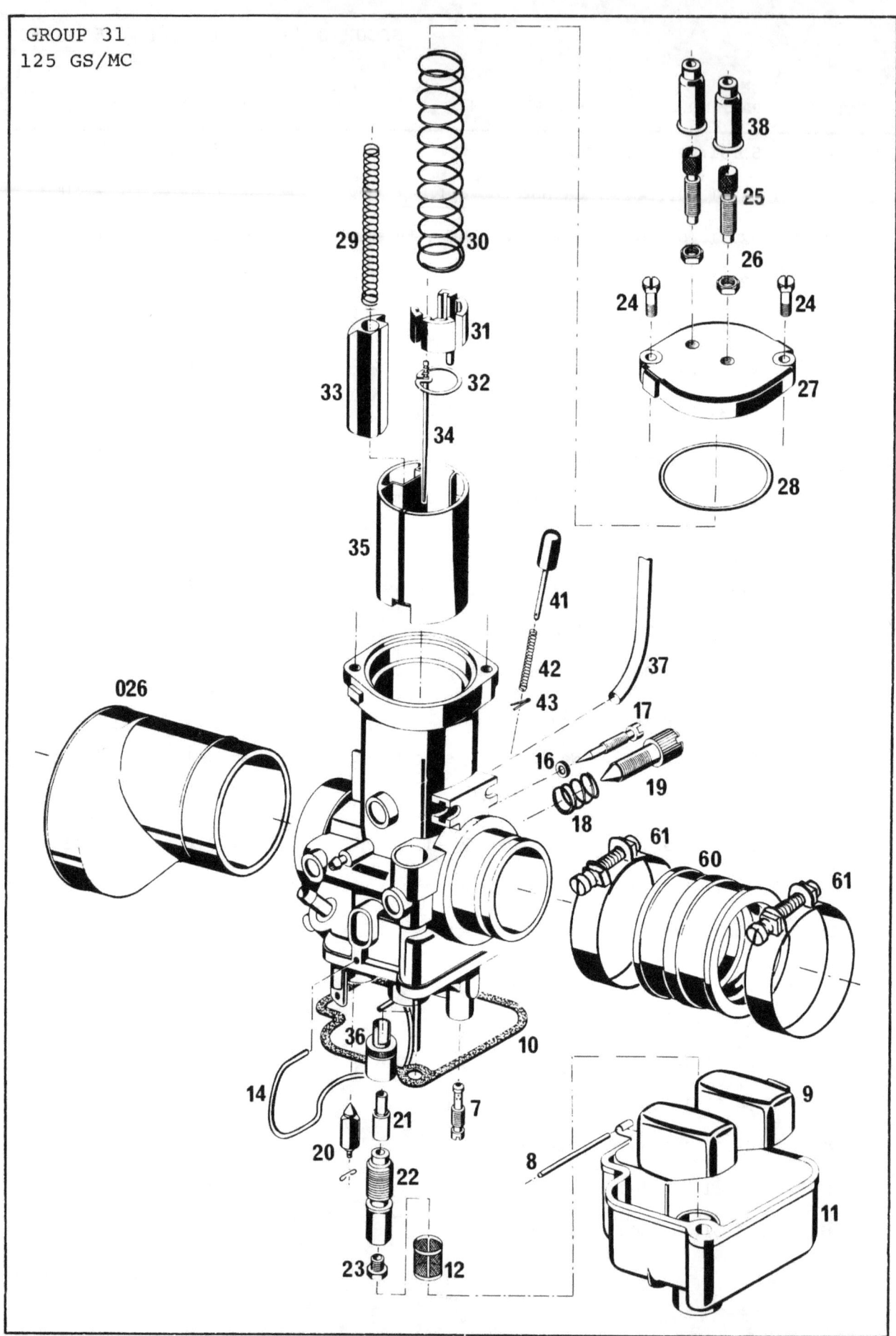

GROUP 31 - CARBURATOR 125 GS/MC

PICTURE	PART NO.	DESCRIPTION		GS	MC
32	54.31.132.000	Needle clip	57-251	1	1
33	54.31.133.000	Air valve	24-055	1	-
34	51.31.134.361	Jet needle, specify size	46-361	1	1
-	51.31.134.362	" " " "	46-362	-	-
-	51.31.134.364	" " " "	46-364	-	-
-	51.31.134.365	" " " "	46-365	-	-
35	51.31.135.210	Throttle valve	22-646/210	1	1
-	51.31.135.220	" "	22-646/220	-	-
-	51.31.135.230	" "	22-646/230	-	-
36	51.31.136.100	Vaporizer	51-555	1	1
37	52.31.137.100	Breather tube	80-711	2	2
38	52.31.138.000	Rubber plug	65-851	2	2
41	51.31.041.000	Tickler	48-830	1	1
42	51.31.042.000	Spring	60-062	1	1
43	51.31.043.000	Pin	49-020	1	1
-	51.30.050.600	Intake adapter		1	1
60	51.30.060.000	Rubber		1	1
61	51.30.061.000	Clamp		2	2
026	51.06.026.100	Air filter boot		1	1

GROUP 31
125 GS/Z

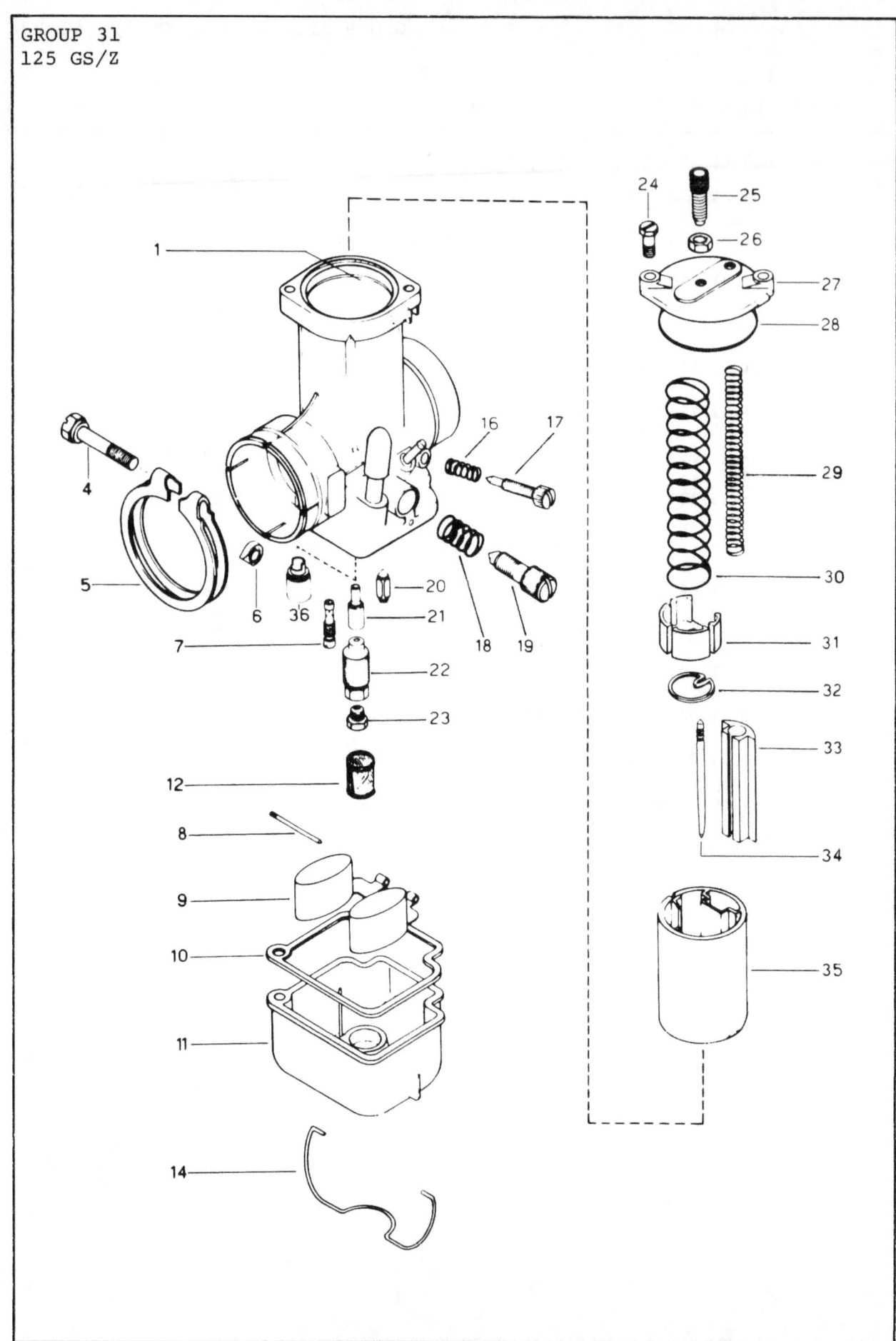

GROUP 31 - CARBURATOR 125 GS/Z

PICTURE	PART NO.	DESCRIPTION	BING NO.	125
-	52.31.101.044	Carburetor cpl.		1
4	52.31.104.000	Pinch bolt	40-626	1
5	52.31.105.000	Clmap	59-114	1
6	52.31.106.000	Nut	42-611	1
7	52.31.107.000	Pilot jet, specify size	44-350	1
8	52.31.108.000	Spindle	52-058	1
9	52.31.109.000	Float	35-300	1
10	52.31.110.000	Seal	65-584	1
11	52.31.111.000	Float chamber body	30-569	1
12	52.31.112.000	Fuel filter	57-701	1
14	52.31.114.000	Float chamber clamp	61-479	1
16	52.31.116.000	Spring	60-160	1
17	51.31.117.000	Pilot air adj. screw	50-023	1
18	52.31.118.000	Spring	60-322	1
19	52.31.119.000	Throttle stop adj. screw	50-072	1
20	51.31.120.000	Float needle	40-405	1
21	52.31.121.000	Needle jet, specify size	45-196	1
22	52.31.122.000	Jet holder	45-420	1
23	52.31.123.000	Jet, specify size	44-051	1
24	52.31.124.000	Top securing bolt	40-518	2
25	52.31.125.000	Cable adjusting screw	50-050	2
26	52.31.126.000	Nut	42-605	2
27	52.31.127.000	Cover	20-642	1
28	52.31.128.000	Rubber seal ring	65-740	1
29	52.31.129.000	Spring	60-194	1
30	51.31.130.000	Spring	60-370	1
31	51.31.131.000	Spring retainer	26-511	1

GROUP 31
125 GS/Z

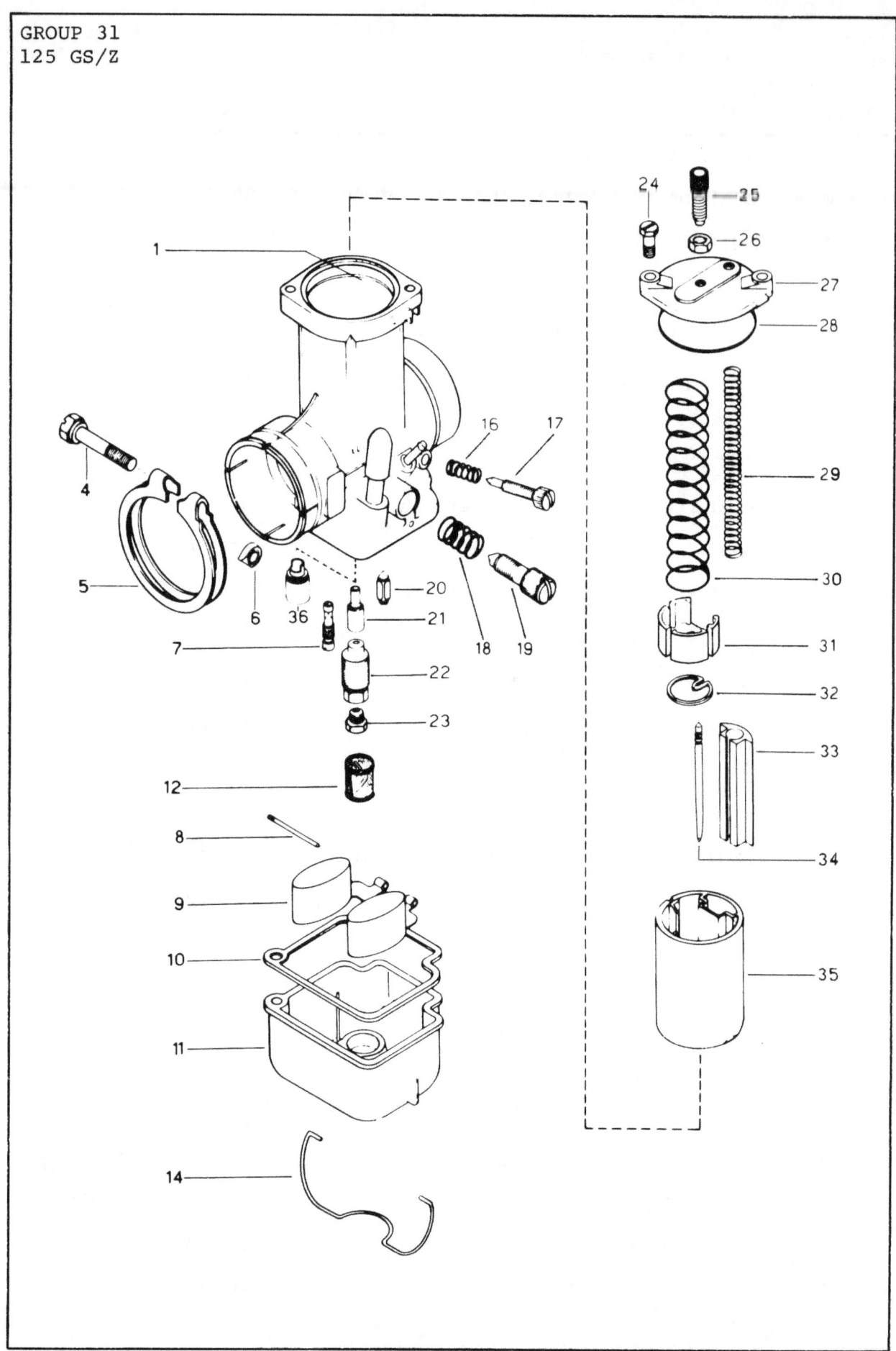

GROUP 31 - CARBURATOR 125 GS/Z

PICTURE	PART NO.	DESCRIPTION	BING NO.	125
32	52.31.132.000	Needle clip	57-253	1
33	52.31.133.000	Air valve	24-056	1
34	52.31.134.001	Jet needle, specify size	46-291	1
-	52.31.134.002	" " " "	46-292	1
-	52.31.134.003	" " " "	46-293	1
-	52.31.135.004	" " " "	46-294	1
35	52.31.135.001	Throttle valve	22-736/1	1
-	52.31.135.002	Throttle valve	22-736/2	1
36	52.31.136.000	Vaporizer	40-404	1
37	52.31.137.000	Breather tube	80-708	1
38	52.31.138.000	Rubber plug	65-851	2
-	51.30.050.600	Intake adapter		1
-	51.30.051.600	Bushing		1
-	51.30.060.000	Rubber		1
-	51.30.061.000	Clamp		2
-	51.06.026.200	Air filter boot		1
-	51.06.029.600	Bushing		1

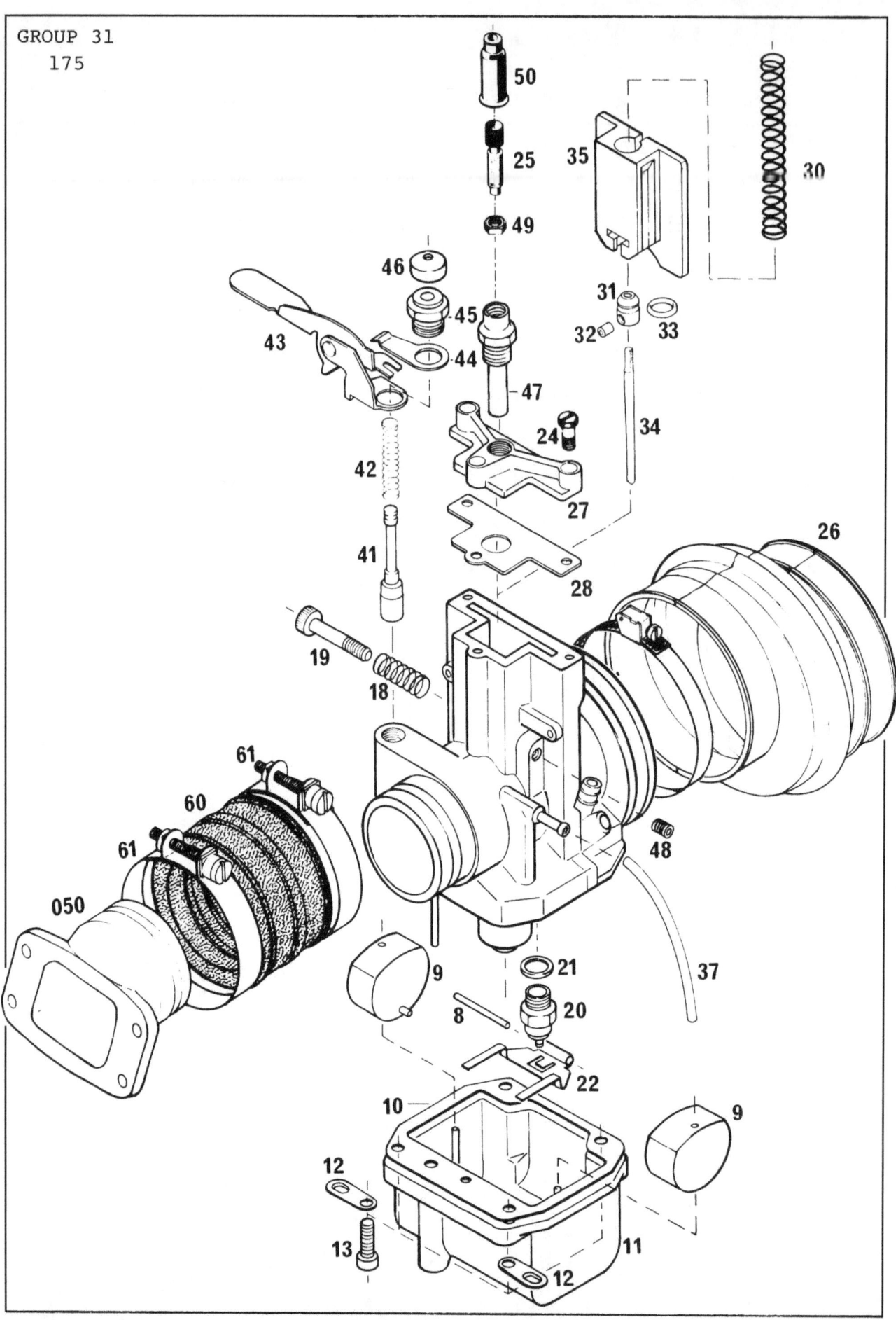

GROUP 31 - CARBURATOR 175

PICTURE	PART NO.	DESCRIPTION	175
	5157	36mm Lectron carburetor cpl.	1
8	HP-5033-1	Pin, float lever	1
9	HP-5028-1	Float Assm.	2
10	HP-5026-1	Bowl gasket	1
11	HP-5389-1	Plastic Bowl Assm.	1
12	HP-5062-1	Vent tube clip	2
13	HP-5025-2	Filister head bowl screw	4
18	HP-5086-2	Idle stop spring	1
19	HP-5057-1	Idle adjusting screw	1
20	HP-5034-1	Needle and seat assm.	1
21	HP-5037-1	Fuel inlet gasket	1
22	HP-5032-1	Float lever	1
24	HP-5019-2	Filister head cover screw	3
25	52.31.125.000	Cable adjusting screw	1
27	52.31.527.000	Cover	1
28	HP-5077-1	Cover gasket	1
30	HP-5048-1	Spring choke	1
31	HP-5063-1	Slide insert	1
32	HP-5043-1	Needle set screw	1
33	HP-5014-1	O-ring	1
34	HP-5400	Metering rod, specify model & size	1
35	HP-5040	Slide ,specify 36mm slide	1
37	HP-5352-1	Vent tube hose	2
41	HP-5045-1	Piston Assm. Choke	1
42	HP-5048-1	Choke spring	1
43	HP-5049-1	Choke lever assm.	1
44	HP-5053-2	Latch choke lever	1
45	HP-5054-1	Choke bushing	1

GROUP 31
175

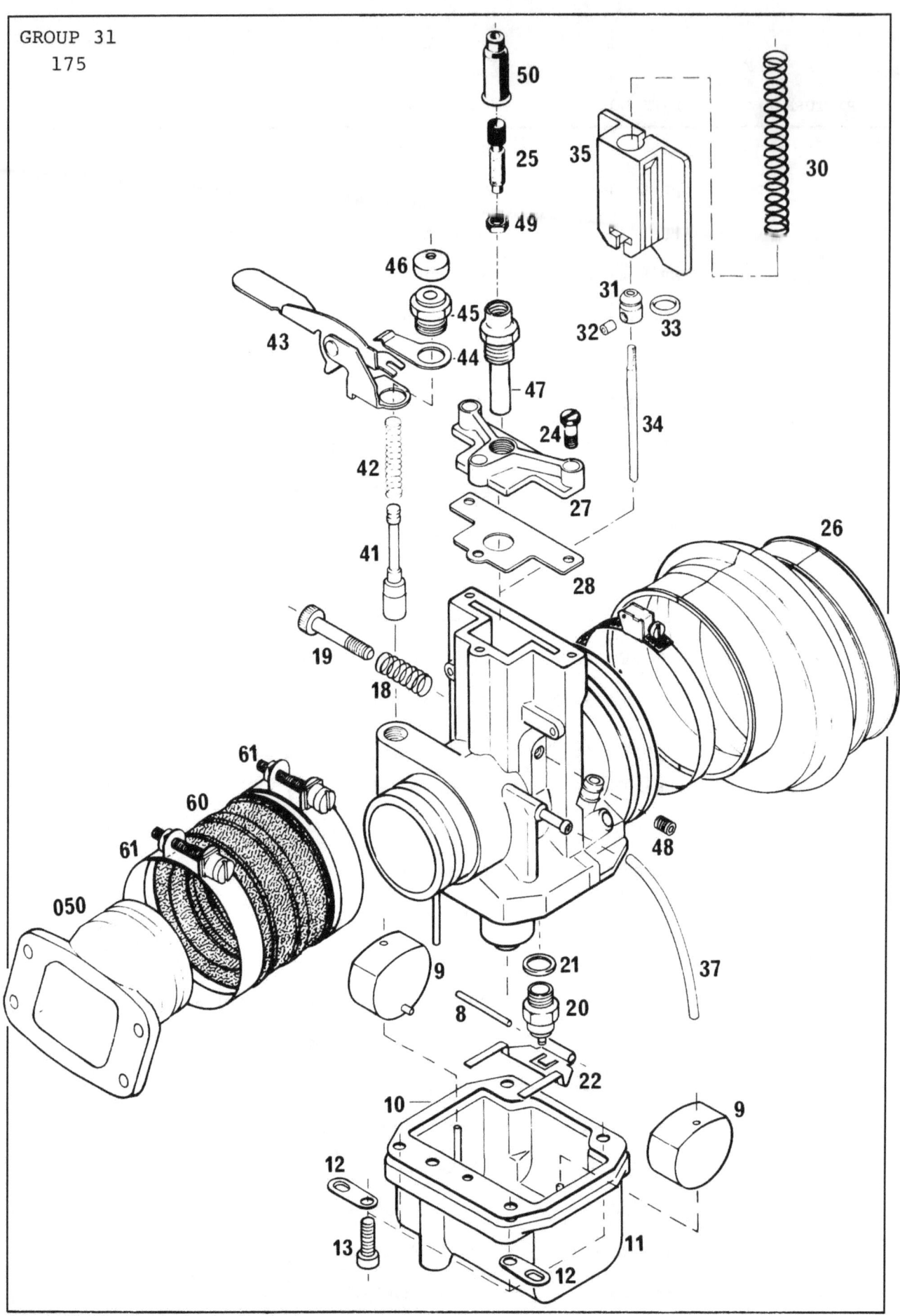

GROUP 31 - CARBURATOR 175

PICTURE	PART NO.	DESCRIPTION	175
46	HP-5055-1	Boot choke	1
47	HP-5335-1	Bushing choke	1
48	HP-5085-1	Set screw	1
49	52.31.126.000	Cable adjusting nut	1
50	52.31.138.000	Weather seal	1
050	52.30.050.500	Intake adapter	1
60	54.30.060.000	Rubber	1
61	51.30.061.000	Clamp	2
26	52.06.026.500	Air filter boot	1

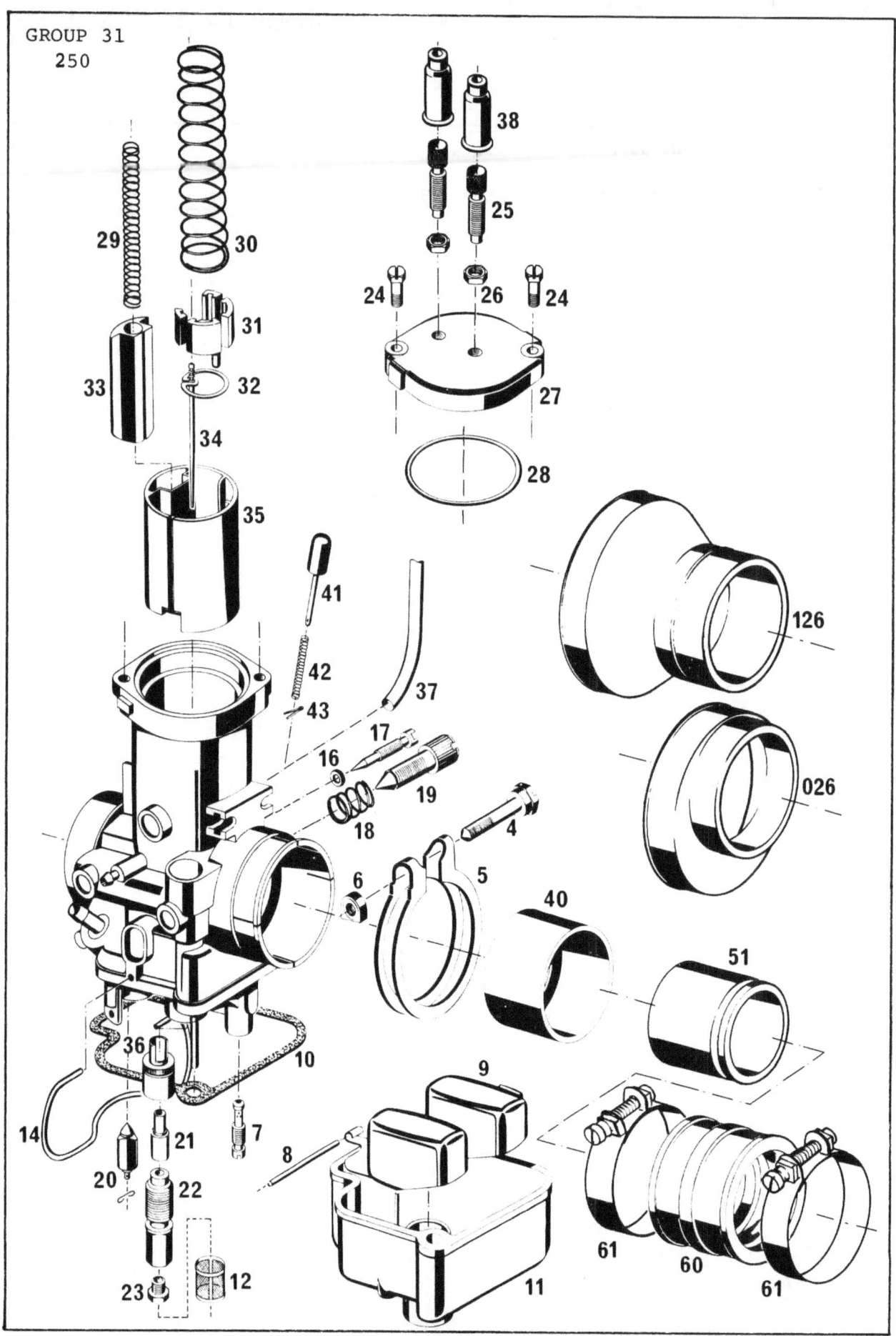

GROUP 31 - CARBURATOR 250

PICTURE	PART NO.	DESCRIPTION	BING NO.	GS	MC
-	54.31.101.144	Carburetor cpl.		1	-
-	54.31.101.244	Carburetor cpl.		-	1
4	52.31.104.100	Pinch bolt	40-636	NB	1
5	54.31.105.100	Clamp	57-130	NB	1
6	52.31.106.100	Nut	42-661	1	1
7	52.31.107.000	Pilot jet, specify size	44-350	1	1
8	52.31.108.000	Spindle	52-058	1	1
9	52.31.109.000	Float	35-300	1	1
10	52.31.110.000	Seal	65-584	1	1
11	52.31.111.000	Float chamber body	30-569	1	1
12	51.31.112.000	Fuel filter	57-706	1	1
14	52.31.114.000	Float chamber clamp	61-479	1	1
16	51.31.116.100	O-ring	65-704	1	1
17	51.31.117.100	Pilot air adj.screw	50-039/101	1	1
18	52.31.118.000	Spring	60-322	1	1
19	52.31.119.000	Throttle stop adj. screw	50-072	1	1
20	51.31.120.100	Float needle	47-968	1	1
21	51.31.121.100	Needle jet, specify size	45-120	1	1
22	51.31.122.100	Jet holder	45-435	1	1
23	52.31.123.000	Jet, specify size	44-051	1	1
24	52.31.124.000	Top securing bolt	40-518	2	2
25	52.31.125.000	Cable adjusting screw	50-050	2	1
26	52.31.126.000	Nut	42-605	2	1
27	51.31.127.100	Cover	20-672/101	1	-
-	51.31.127.200	Cover		-	1
28	54.31.128.000	Rubber seal ring	65-745	1	1
29	54.31.129.000	Spring	60-195	1	-

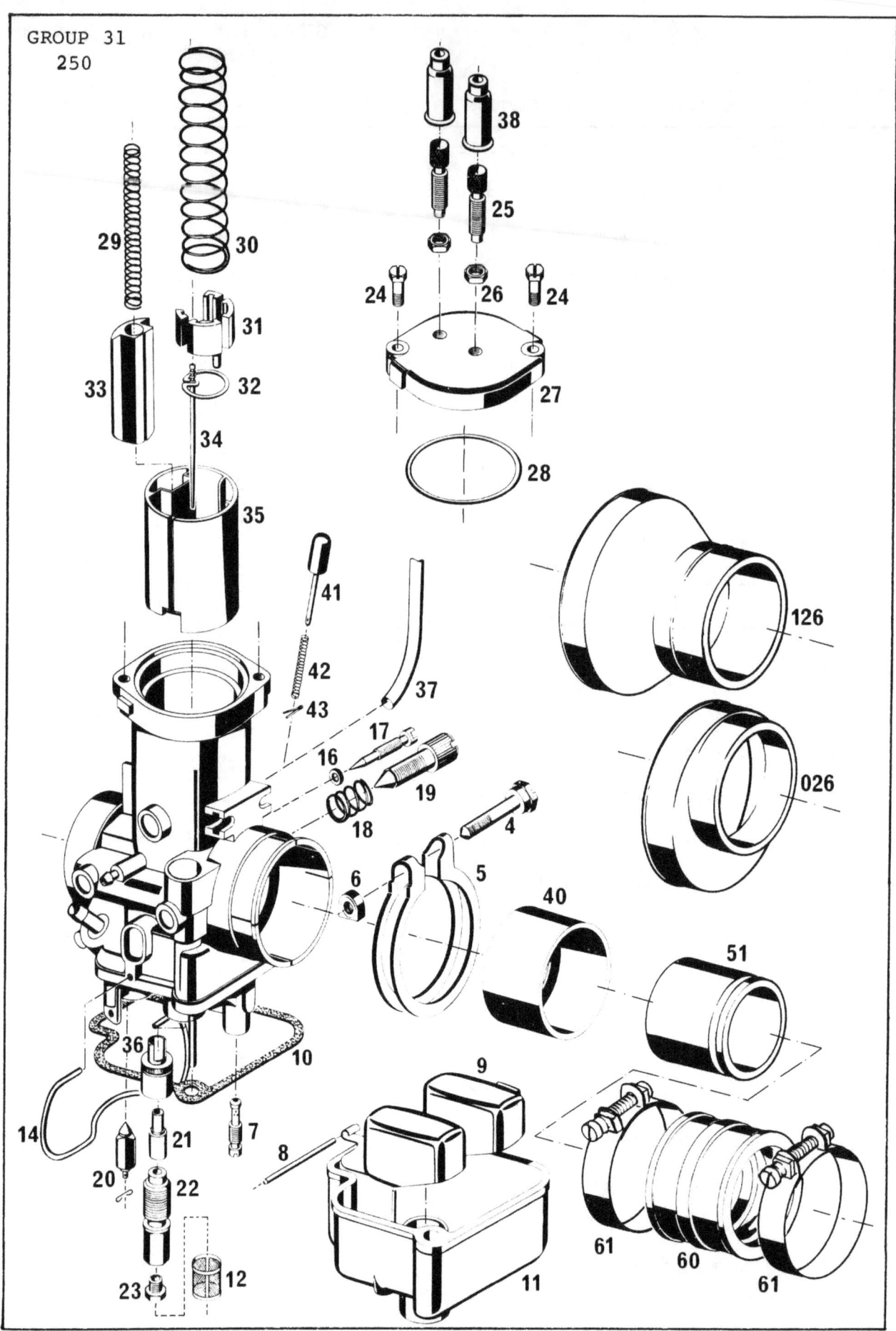

GROUP 31 - CARBURATOR 250

PICTURE	PART NO.	DESCRIPTION	BING NO.	GS	MC
30	51.31.130.100	Spring	60-434	1	1
31	55.31.131.000	Spring retainer	26-512	1	1
32	54.31.132.000	Needle clip	57-251	1	1
33	54.31.133.000	Air valve	24-055	1	-
34	51.31.134.361	Jet needle, specify size	46-361	1	1
-	51.31.134.362	" " " "	46-362	1	1
-	51.31.134.364	" " " "	46-364	1	1
-	51.31.134.365	" " " "	46-365	1	1
35	51.31.135.210	Throttle valve	22-646-210	1	1
-	51.31.135.220	" "	22-646-220	1	1
-	51.31.135.230	" "	22-646-230	1	1
36	54.31.136.100	Vaporizer	51-552	1	1
41	51.31.041.000	Tickler	48-830	1	1
42	51.31.042.000	Spring	60-062	1	1
43	51.31.043.000	Pin	49-020	1	1
-	52.31.137.100	Breather tube	80-711	2	2
40	54.31.140.100	Isolating bushing	66-639	NB	NB
38	52.31.138.000	Rubber plug		2	1
-	54.30.050.600	Intake adapter		1	-
-	54.30.150.500	Intake adapter		-	1
60	54.30.060.000	Rubber		1	-
61	51.30.061.000	Clamp		2	2
026	54.06.026.500	Air filter boot		1	-
126	55.06.026.000	Air filter boot		-	1
51	54.30.051.500	Bushing		1	-

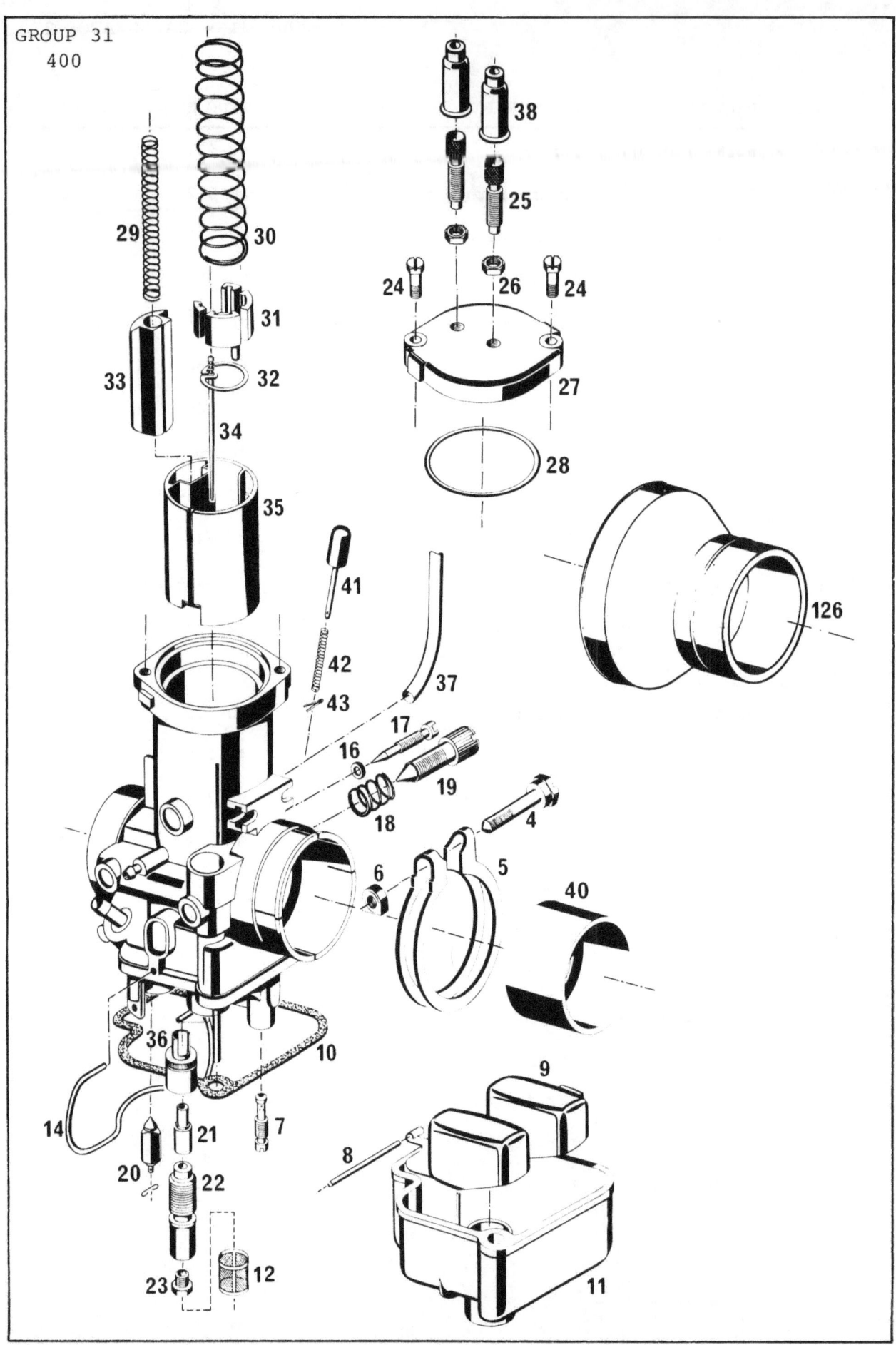

GROUP 31
400

42

GROUP 31 - CARBURATOR 400

PICTURE	PART NO.	DESCRIPTION	BING NO.	GS	MC
-	55.31.101.144	Carburetor cpl.		1	1
4	52.31.104.100	Pinch bolt	40-636	1	1
5	54.31.105.100	Clamp	59-130	1	1
6	52.31.106.100	Nut	42-661	1	1
7	52.31.107.000	Pilot jet, specify size	44-350	1	1
8	52.31.108.000	Spindle	52-058	1	1
9	52.31.109.000	Float	35-300	1	1
10	52.31.110.000	Seal	65-584	1	1
11	51.31.111.100	Float chamber body	30-569	1	1
12	51.31.112.000	Fuel filter	57-706	1	1
14	52.31.114.000	Float chamber clamp	61-479	1	1
16	51.31.116.100	O-ring	65-704	1	1
17	51.31.117.100	Pilot air adj. screw	50-039/101	1	1
18	52.31.118.000	Spring	60-322	1	1
19	52.31.119.000	Throttle stop adj. screw	50-072	1	1
20	51.31.120.100	Float needle	47-968	1	1
21	51.31.121.100	Needle jet, specify size	45-120	1	1
22	51.31.122.100	Jet holder	45-435	1	1
23	52.31.123.000	Jet specify size	44-051	1	1
24	52.31.124.000	Top securing bolt	40-518	2	2
25	52.31.125.000	Cable adjusting screw	50-050	2	1
26	52.31.126.000	Nut	42-605	2	1
27	51.31.127.100	Cover	20-672/101	1	-
-	51.31.127.200	Cover		-	1
28	54.31.128.000	Rubber seal ring	65-745	1	1
29	54.31.129.000	Spring	60-195	1	-
30	51.31.130.100	Spring	60-434	1	1

GROUP 31
400

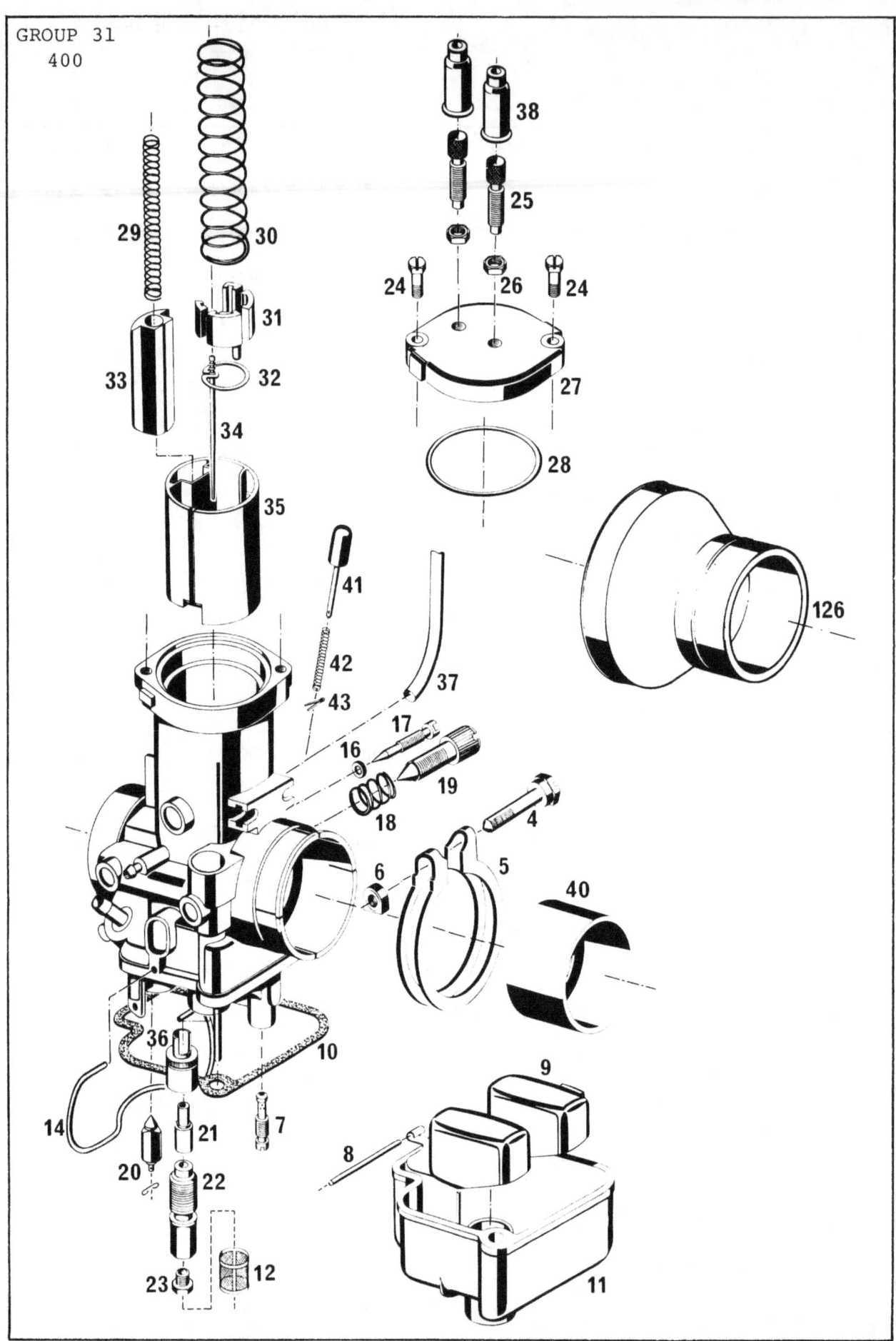

44

GROUP 31 - CARBURATOR 400

PICTURE	PART NO.	DESCRIPTION	BING NO.	GS	MC
31	55.31.131.000	Spring retainer	26-512	1	1
32	54.31.132.000	Needle clip	57-251	1	1
33	54.31.133.000	Air valve	24-055	1	-
34	51.31.134.361	Jet needle, specify size	46-361	1	1
-	51.31.134.362	" " " "	46-362	1	1
-	51.31.134.364	" " " "	46-364	1	1
-	51.31.134.365	" " " "	46-365	1	1
35	51.31.135.210	Throttle valve	22-646/210	1	1
-	51.31.135.220	" "	22-646/220	1	1
-	51.31.135.230	" "	22-646/230	1	1
36	55.31.136.100	Vaporizer	51-554	1	1
37	52.31.137.100	Breather tube	80-711	2	2
38	52.31.138.000	Rubber plug	65-851	2	2
41	51.31.041.000	Tickler	48-830	1	1
42	51.31.042.000	Spring	60-062	1	1
43	51.31.043.000	Pin	49-020	1	1
40	54.31.140.100	Isolating bushing	66-639	1	1
-	55.30.050.500	Intake adapter		1	-
-	55.30.150.500	Intake adapter		-	1
-	55.06.026.000	Air filter boot		1	1

GROUP 31

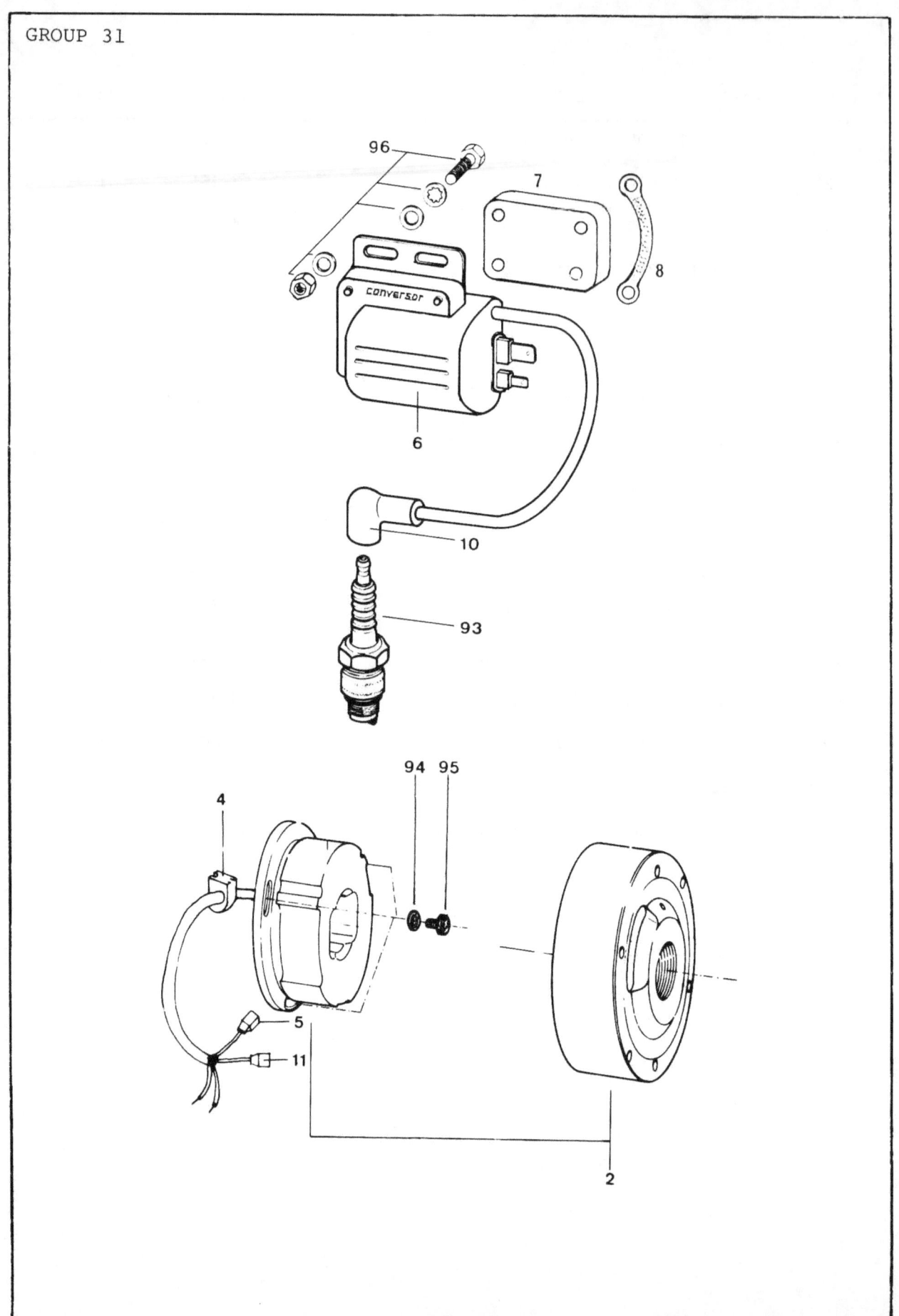

GROUP 31 - CARBURATOR 400

PICTURE	PART NO.	DESCRIPTION	BING NO.	GS	MC
31	55.31.131.000	Spring retainer	26-512	1	1
32	54.31.132.000	Needle clip	57-251	1	1
33	54.31.133.000	Air valve	24-055	1	-
34	51.31.134.361	Jet needle, specify size	46-361	1	1
-	51.31.134.362	" " " "	46-362	1	1
-	51.31.134.364	" " " "	46-364	1	1
-	51.31.134.365	" " " "	46-365	1	1
35	51.31.135.210	Throttle valve	22-646/210	1	1
-	51.31.135.220	" "	22-646/220	1	1
-	51.31.135.230	" "	22-646/230	1	1
36	55.31.136.100	Vaporizer	51-554	1	1
37	52.31.137.100	Breather tube	80-711	2	2
38	52.31.138.000	Rubber plug	65-851	2	2
41	51.31.041.000	Tickler	48-830	1	1
42	51.31.042.000	Spring	60-062	1	1
43	51.31.043.000	Pin	49-020	1	1
40	54.31.140.100	Isolating bushing	66-639	1	1
-	55.30.050.500	Intake adapter		1	-
-	55.30.150.500	Intake adapter		-	1
-	55.06.026.000	Air filter boot		1	1

GROUP 31

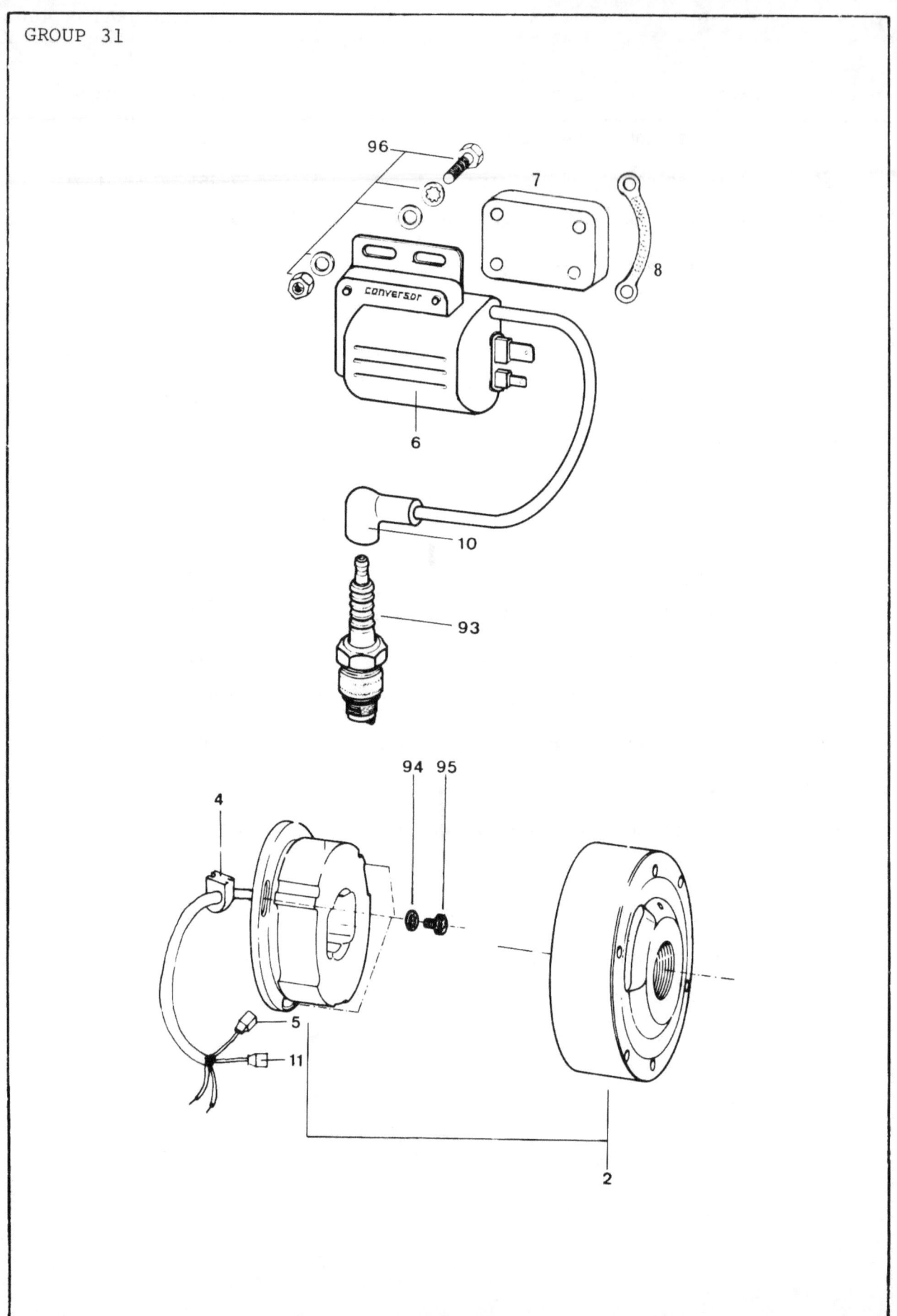

GROUP 31 - IGNITION

PICTURE	PART NO.	DESCRIPTION	125	175	250	400
-	51.31.001.200	Ignition cpl. 6 V 35/5/21 W with ignition coil (type 9600-162-1) flywheel 116mm	1	1	1	1
2	51.31.002.000	Ignition cpl. wo/ignition coil (red protection caps)	1	1	1	1
4	51.31.004.000	Rubber cable grommet	1	1	1	1
5	51.31.005.000	Receptable, Small	1	1	1	1
6	51.31.006.200	Ignition coil, red ignition cable (suitable for all ignitions)	1	1	1	1
7	51.31.007.000	Ignition coil bracket	1	1	1	1
8	51.31.008.000	Ground cable	1	1	1	1
10	51.31.010.100	Spark plug protector	1	1	1	1
11	51.31.011.000	Receptacle, Large	1	1	1	1
93	51.31.093.100	Spark plug	1	1	1	1
94	0137 040000	Spring washer A 4	3	3	3	3
95	0085 040123	Flat head screw AM 4x12	3	3	3	3
96	51.31.096.000	Hexagon head screw M 6x20 cpl.	4	4	4	4

GROUP 32

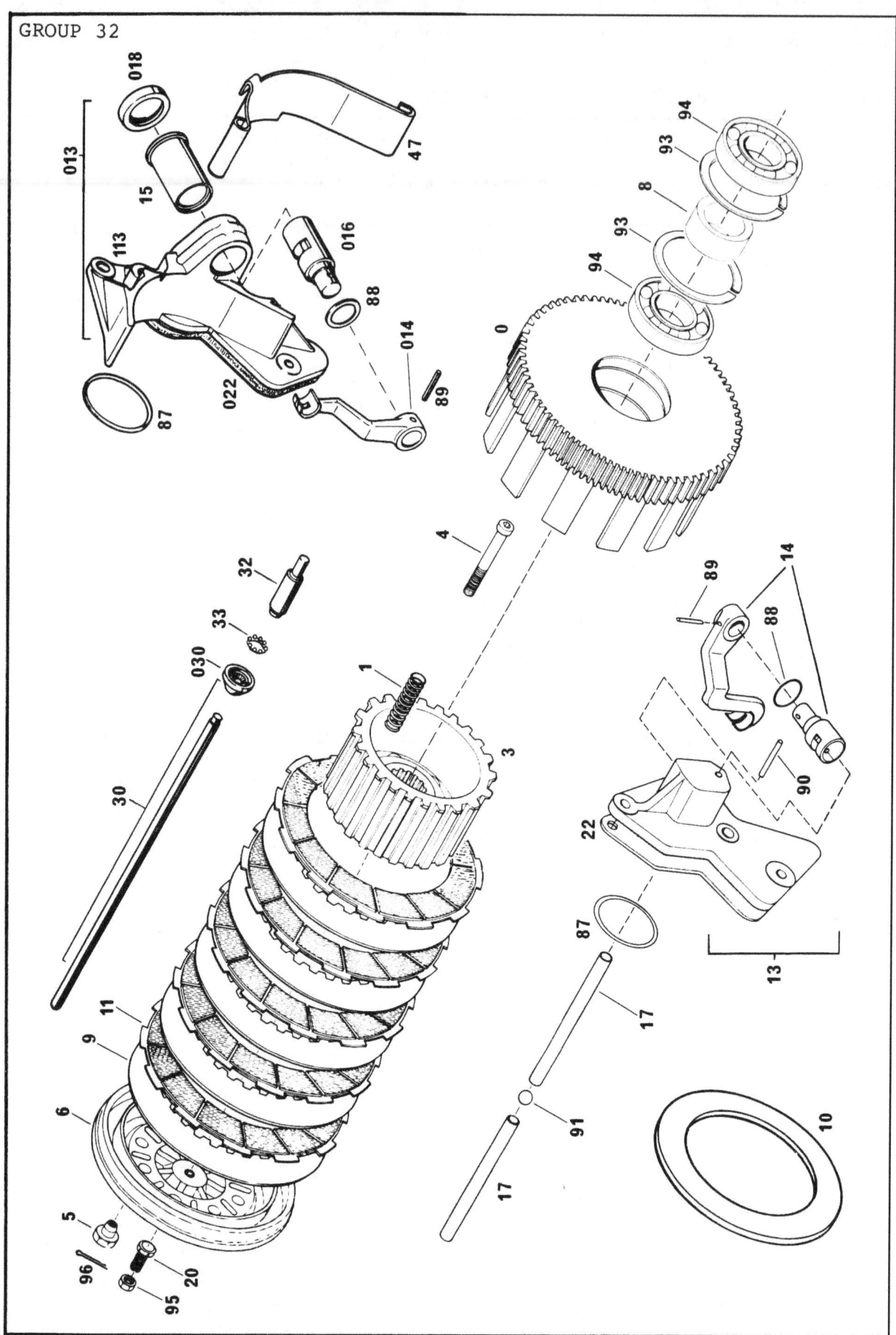

48

GROUP 32 - CLUTCH

PICTURE	PART NO.	DESCRIPTION	125	175	250 GS	250 MC	400
0	51.32.000.644	Outer clutch hub 73T with pinion 20T	1	-	-	-	-
-	51.32.000.544	Outer clutch hub 69T with pinion 25T	-	1	-	-	-
-	54.32.000.544	Outer clutch hub 69T with pinion 25T	-	-	1	1	1
1	51.32.001.120	Clutch spring 1.5mm	8	8	-	-	-
-	51.32.001.140	Clutch spring 1.7mm	-	-	8	8	8
3	51.32.003.500	Inner Clutch hub, Alu	1	-	-	-	-
-	51.32.003.200	Inner clutch hub	-	1	1	1	1
4	51.32.004.100	Spring bolt	8	8	8	8	8
5	51.32.005.100	Spring nut	8	8	8	8	8
6	51.32.006.500	Pressure plate	1	1	-	-	-
-	54.32.006.000	Pressure plate	-	-	1	1	1
8	51.32.008.100	Distance bushing	1	1	1	1	1
9	51.32.009.500	Alu disc	5	-	-	-	-
-	51.32.009.100	Steel disc	-	5	8	8	9
10	51.32.010.100	Bottom ring Alu	-	-	1	-	-
11	51.32.011.011	Clutch disc, organic	5	-	-	-	-
-	54.32.011.250	Clutch disc 2.5mm	-	-	7	-	-
-	55.32.011.250	Clutch disc 2.0mm	-	-	-	-	8
-	52.32.011.000	Clutch disc 3.5mm	-	5	-	6	-
13	51.32.013.300	Bearing cover cpl.	1	1	1	1	-
14	51.32.014.200	Disengaging lever cpl. with shaft	1	1	1	1	-
17	51.32.017.100	Pushrod	2	2	2	2	-
20	51.32.020.100	Pressure bolt heat treating	1	1	1	1	1
22	51.32.022.200	Gasket for bearing cover	1	1	1	1	1
87	0770 021260	O-ring 2-126	1	1	1	1	1
88	0770 021120	O-ring 2-112	1	1	1	1	1

GROUP 32

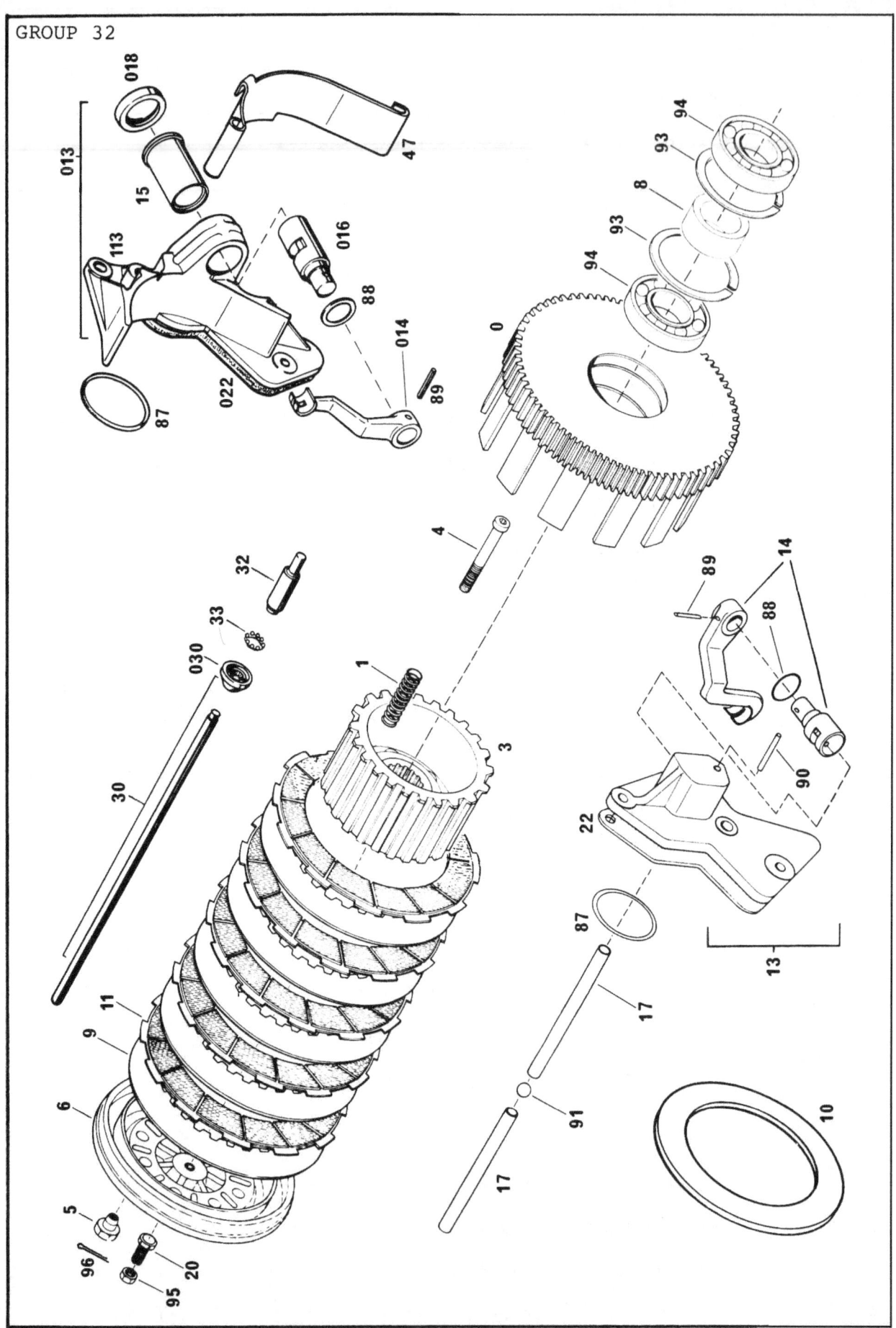

GROUP 32 - CLUTCH

PICTURE	PART NO.	DESCRIPTION	125	175	250 GS	250 MC	400
89	0402 041580	Bearing needle 4 DIN 5402	1	1	1	1	1
90	04020 042380	Bearing needle 4 DIN 5402	1	1	1	1	1
91	0401 060000	Ball 6 DIN 5401	1	1	1	1	1
93	52.32.093.000	Circlip SB 47	2	2	2	2	2
94	0625 160050	Ball bearing 16005 C 3 SV 41	2	2	2	2	2
95	0439 050002	Hexagon nut M 5 DIN 439	1	1	1	1	1
96	0094 010150	Pin 1x15	8	8	8	8	8
113	54.32.013.000	Bearing cover, loose	1	1	1	1	1
013	54.32.013.044	Bearing cover cpl.	1	1	1	1	1
014	54.32.014.000	Desengaging lever	1	1	1	1	1
015	54.32.015.000	Bushing for disengaging shaft	1	1	1	1	1
016	54.32.016.000	Disengaging shaft	1	1	1	1	1
018	54.32.018.000	Plastic cap	1	1	1	1	1
22	54.32.022.000	Gasket	1	1	1	1	1
30	54.32.030.000	Pushrod with part 030	1	1	1	1	1
030	54.32.030.500	Bearing box	1	1	1	1	1
32	54.32.032.000	Pressure bolt	1	1	1	1	1
33	54.32.033.000	Ball bearing	1	1	1	1	1
47	54.30.047.000	Crank case protector	1	1	1	1	1
48	54.32.048.000	Shim 12.2x20x0.4	1	1	1	1	1
49	0912 060452	Allen head screw M 6x45	1	1	1	1	1

GROUP 33
125/175

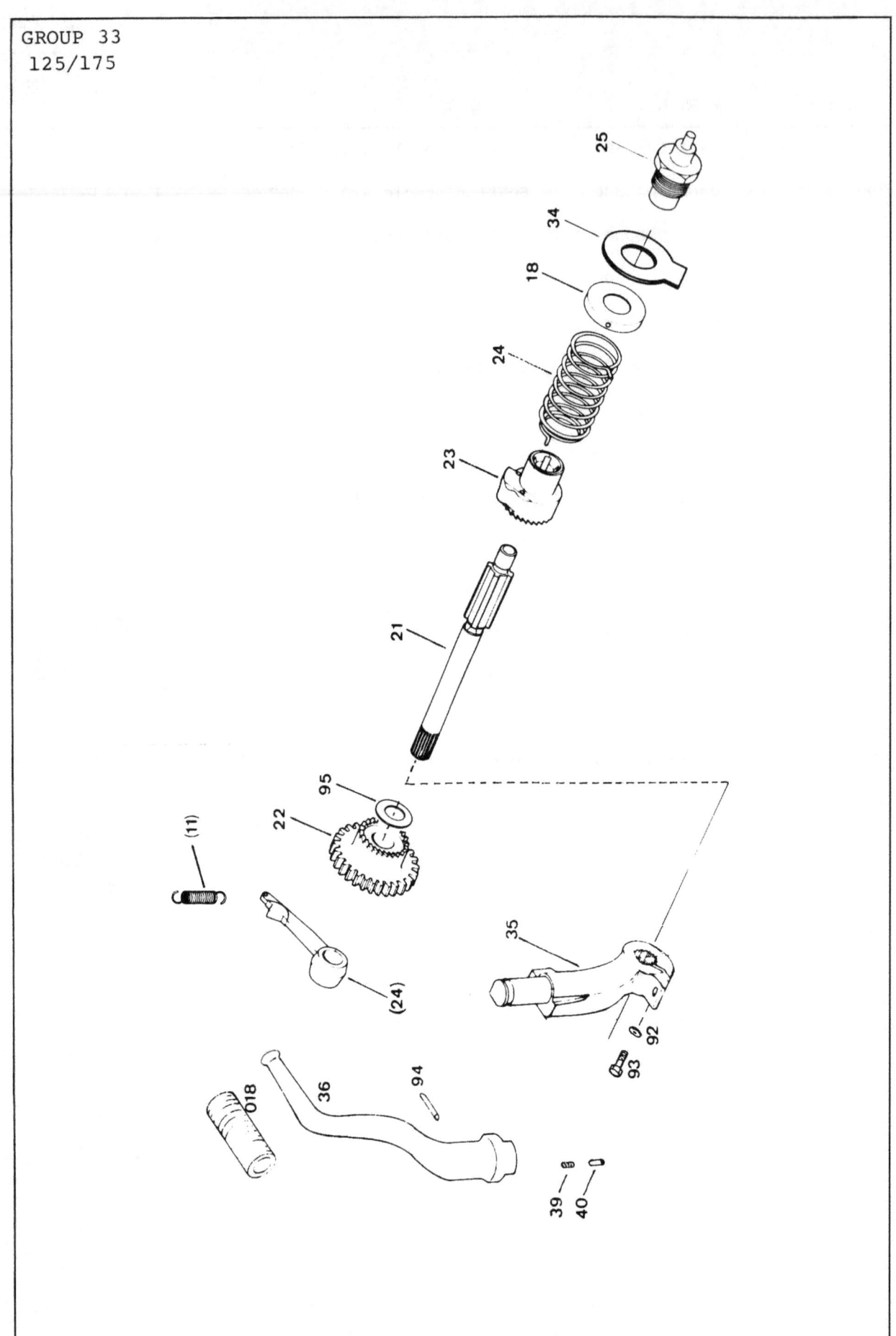

GROUP 33 - KICKSTARTER 125/175

PICTURE	PART NO.	DESCRIPTION	
18	51.33.018.000	Spring cup	1
018	20.05.018.000	Kickstarter rubber	1
21	51.33.021.000	Kickstarter shaft	1
22	51.33.022.000	Kickstarter gear	1
23	51.33.023.000	Kickstarter ratchet	1
24	51.33.024.100	Kickstarter spring	1
25	51.33.025.000	Screw plug	1
34	51.33.034.000	Sheet metal lock washer 1mm	NB
-	51.33.034.100	Sheet metal lock washer 0.75mm	NB
-	51.33.034.200	Sheet metal lock washer 0.5mm	NB
-	52.33.036.144	Kickstarter cpl.	1
35	52.33.035.100	Lower part of kickstarter	1
36	52.33.036.100	Upper part of kickstarter	1
39	20.05.021.000	Locating spring	1
40	20.05.022.000	Locating pin	1
92	0137 060000	Spring washer B 6 DIN 127	1
93	0931 060253	Hexagon head screw M 6x25	1
94	0481 040180	Pin 4x18 DIN 1481	1
95	51.33.095.000	Thrust washer	1

GROUP 33
250/400

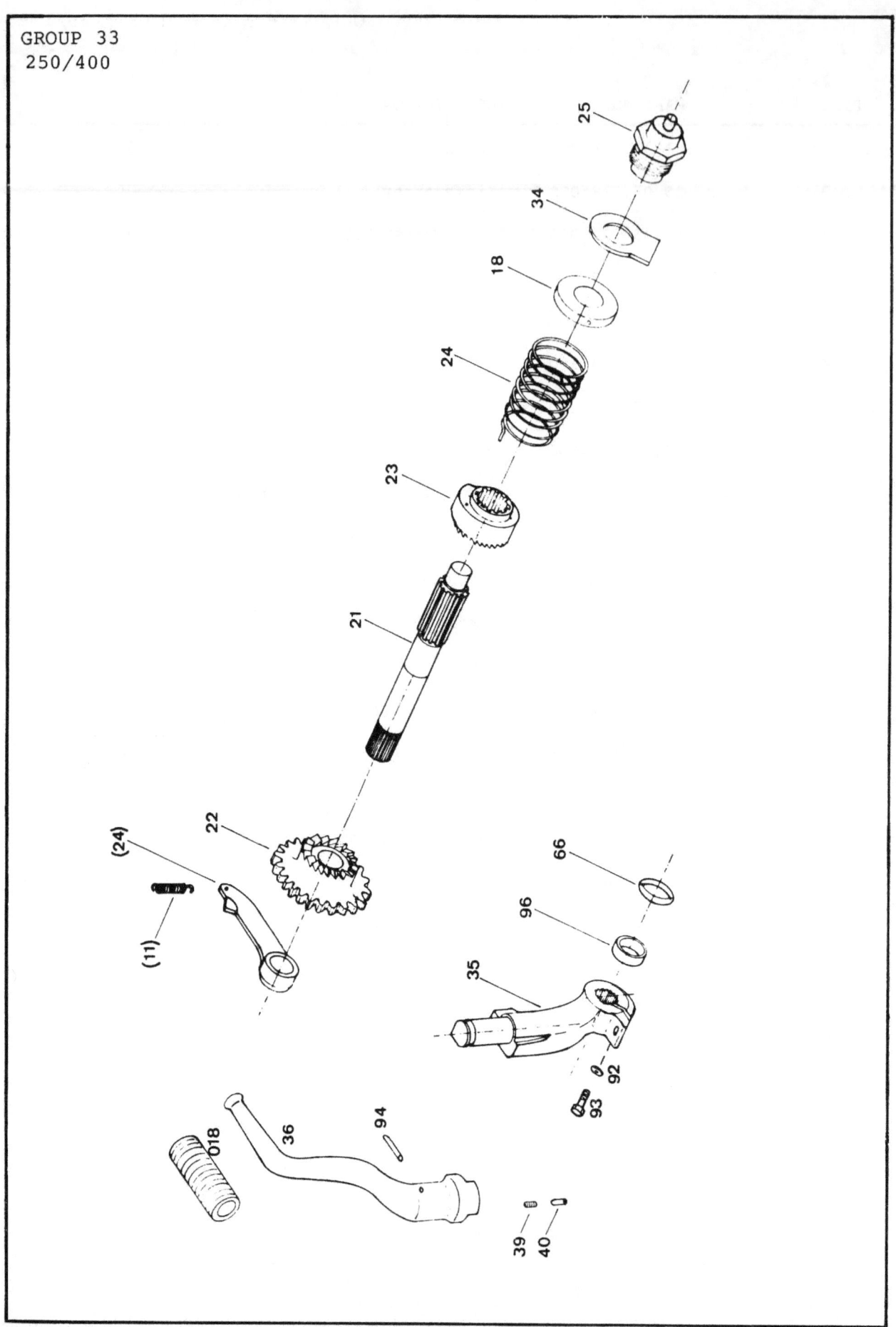

GROUP 33 - KICKSTARTER 250/400

PICTURE	PART NO.	DESCRIPTION	250	400
18	55.33.018.000	Spring cup	1	1
018	20.05.018.000	Kickstarter rubber	1	1
21	55.33.021.100	Kickstarter shaft	1	1
22	55.33.022.000	Kickstarter gear	1	1
23	55.33.023.200	Kickstarter ratchet	1	1
24	51.33.024.100	Kickstarter spring	1	1
25	55.33.025.000	Screw plug	1	1
34	51.33.034.000	Sheet metal lock washer 1mm	NB	NB
-	51.33.034.100	Sheet metal lock washer 0.75mm	NB	NB
-	51.33.034.200	Sheet metal lock washer 0.5mm	NB	NB
39	20.05.021.000	Locating spring	1	1
-	55.33.036.144	Kickstarter cpl.	-	1
35	54.33.035.100	Lower part of kickstarter	1	1
36	54.33.036.100	Upper part of kickstarter	1	1
40	20.05.022.000	Locating pin	1	1
66	0770 160030	O-ring 16x3 DIN 3770	1	1
92	0137 060000	Spring washer B 6 DIN 127	1	1
93	0931 060253	Hexagon head screw M 6x25	1	1
94	0481 040180	Pin 4x18 DIN 1481	1	1
96	55.33.096.000	Bushing	1	1

GROUP 33/I

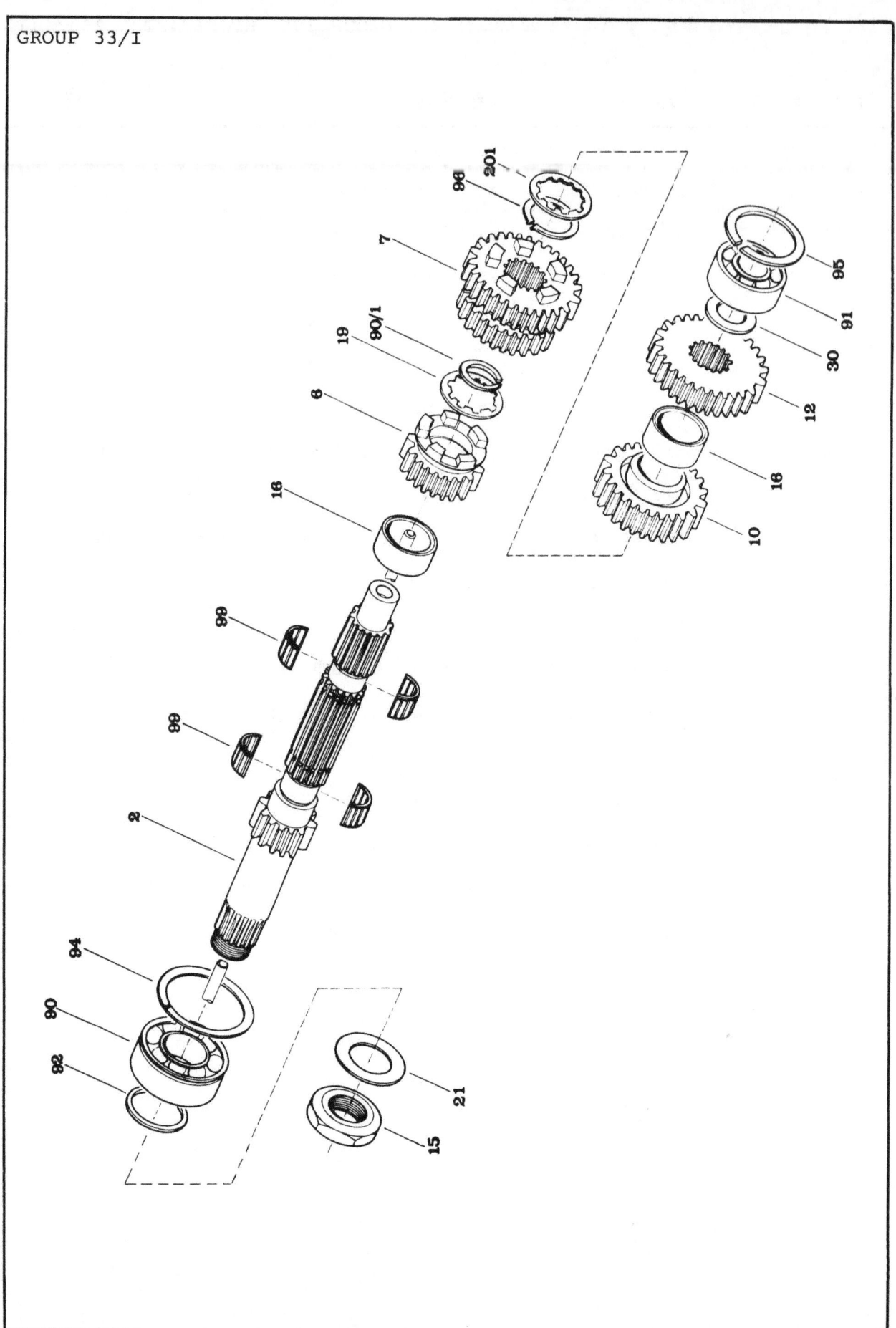

GROUP 33/1 - TRANSMISSION I

PICTURE	PART NO.	DESCRIPTION	125	175	250	400
2	54.33.002.000	Mainshaft	1	1	1	1
6	54.33.006.000	2nd gear - mainshaft	1	1	1	1
7	54.33.007.000	3rd/5th gear mainshaft	1	1	1	1
10	54.33.010.000	4th gear mainshaft	1	1	1	1
12	54.33.012.200	6th gear mainshaft	NB	1	1	1
-	54.33.014.000	6th gear mainshaft 29T	1	-	-	-
15	51.32.015.100	Nut M 22x1.5	1	1	1	1
16	51.33.016.200	Spacer	2	2	2	2
19	51.33.019.100	Thrust washer	1	1	1	1
201	51.33.020.100	Thrust washer	1	1	1	1
21	51.32.021.000	Flat washer	1	1	1	1
30	51.33.030.000	Thrust washer	1	1	1	1
90	0625 062053	Ball bearing 6205 NC 3, SV 41	1	1	1	1
90/1	51.33.090.100	Circlip SW 25	1	1	1	1
91	0625 062030	Ball bearing 6203 C3,SV 41 DIN 625	1	1	1	1
92	51.33.020.000	Spacer washer 32	1	1	1	1
94	52.33.094.000	Circlip SP 52 DIN 5417	1	1	1	1
95	52.33.095.000	Circlip SB 40	1	1	1	1
96	52.33.096.000	Circlip WA 985	1	1	1	1
99	52.33.099.000	Needle cage	2	2	2	2

GROUP 33/II

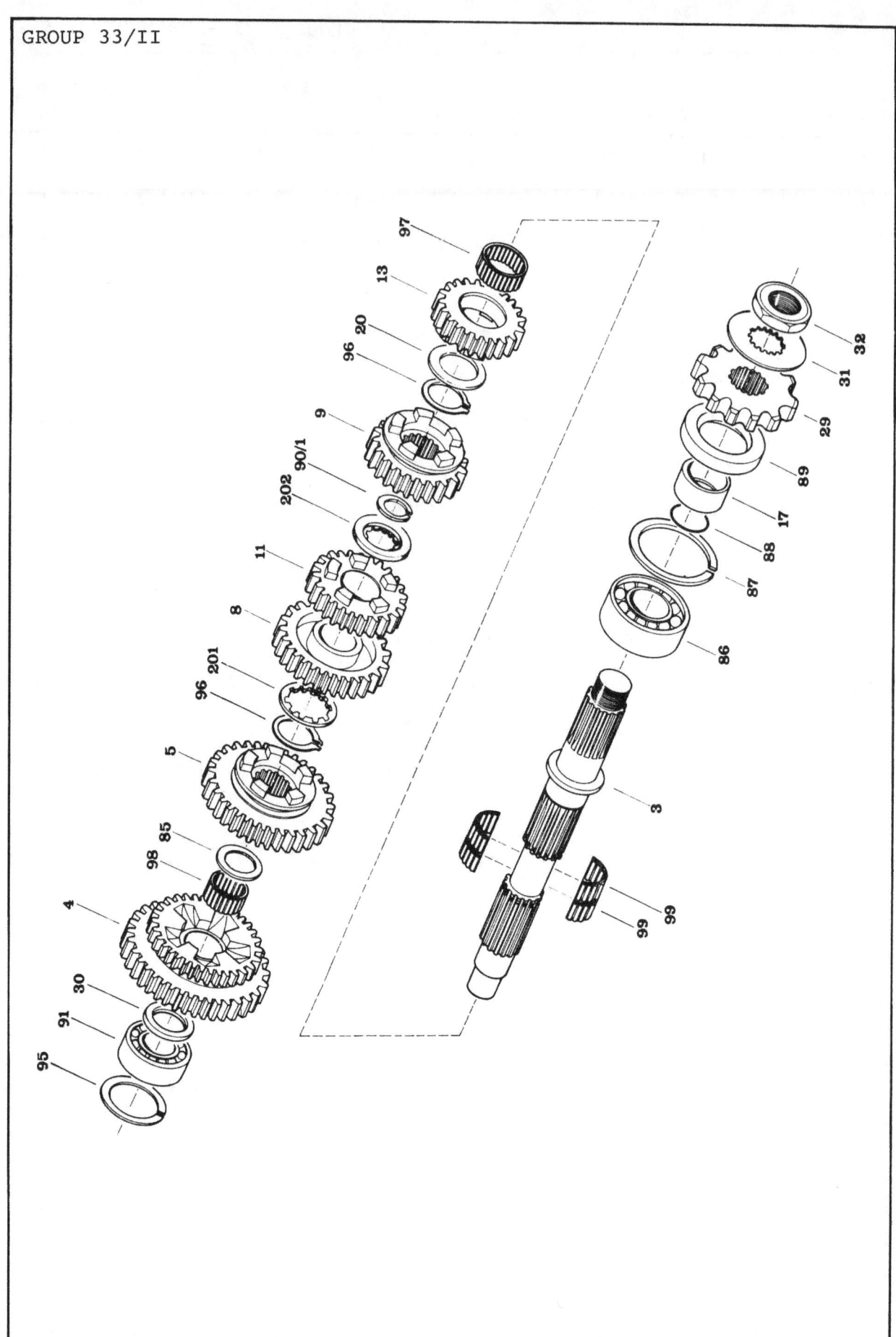

GROUP 33/II - TRANSMISSION II

PICTURE	PART NO.	DESCRIPTION	125	175	250	400
3	54.33.003.000	Counter shaft	1	1	1	1
4	54.33.004.100	1st gear counter shaft	1	1	1	1
5	54.33.005.000	2nd gear counter shaft	1	1	1	1
8	54.33.008.000	3rd gear counter shaft	1	1	1	1
9	54.33.009.000	4th gear counter shaft	1	1	1	1
11	54.33.011.000	5th gear counter shaft	1	1	1	1
13	54.33.013.200	6th gear counter shaft	1	1	1	1
17	51.33.017.000	Spacer	1	1	1	1
201	51.33.020.100	Thrust washer	1	1	1	1
202	51.33.020.200	Thrust washer	1	1	1	1
20	51.33.020.000	Supporting disc 32	1	1	1	1
29	54.33.029.040	Sprocket 11T 3/8 x 5/8	-	-	NB	NB
-	54.33.029.050	Sprocket 12 T	-	-	1	1
-	54.33.029.060	Sprocket 13 T	-	-	NB	NB
-	54.33.029.070	Sprocket 14 T	-	-	NB	NB
-	54.33.029.080	Sprocket 15 T	-	-	NB	NB
-	51.33.029.512	Sprocket 12 T	1	1	-	-
-	51.33.029.513	Sprocket 13 T	NB	NB	-	-
-	51.33.029.514	Sprocket 14 T	NB	NB	-	-
-	51.33.029.515	Sprocket 15 T	NB	NB	-	-
30	51.33.030.000	Thrust washer	1	1	1	1
31	51.33.031.000	Sheet metal lock washer	1	1	1	1
32	51.33.032.000	Nut M 20x1.5	1	1	1	1
85	52.33.088.000	Supporting disc	1	1	1	1
86	0625 062050	Ball bearing 6205 C3, SV 41 DIN 625	1	1	1	1
87	52.33.087.000	Circlip SB 52	1	1	1	1
88	0770 020220	O-ring 2-22	1	1	1	1
89	0760 325270	Radial seal ring BA 32x52x7	1	1	1	1

GROUP 33/II

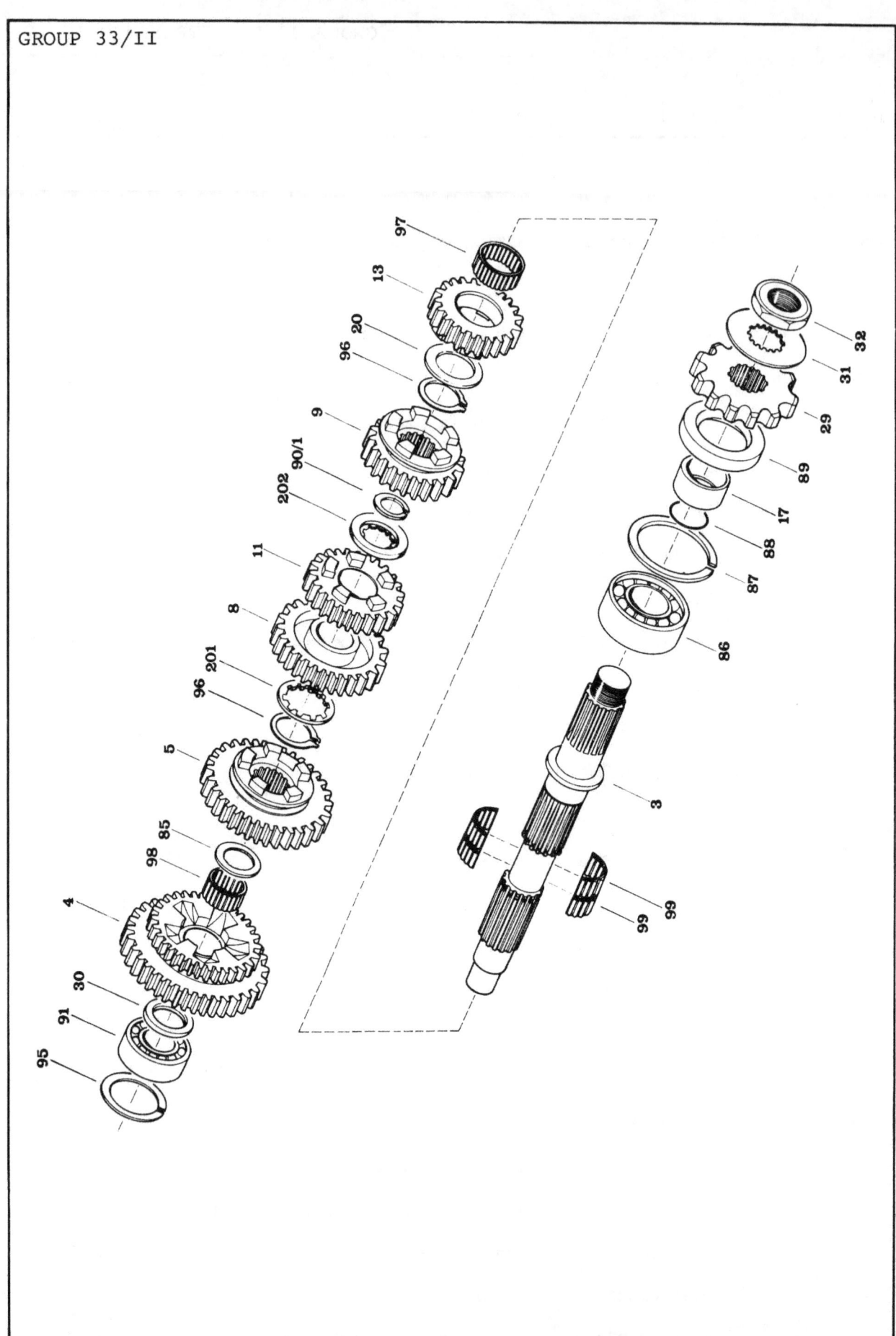

GROUP 33/II - TRANSMISSION II

PICTURE	PART NO.	DESCRIPTION	125	175	250	400
90/1	52.33.090.100	Circlip SW 25	1	1	1	1
91	0625 062030	Ball bearing 6203 C3, SV 41 DIN 625	1	1	1	1
95	52.33.095.000	Circlip	1	1	1	1
97	52.33.097.000	Needle cage	1	1	1	1
98	52.33.098.000	Needle cage	1	1	1	1
99	52.33.099.000	Needle cage	2	2	2	2
-	51.33.029.014	Sprocket 14 T 1/2 x 5/16	NB	-	-	-
-	51.33.029.015	Sprocket 15 T	NB	-	-	-
-	51.33.029.016	Sprocket 16 T	NB	-	-	-

GROUP 34/I

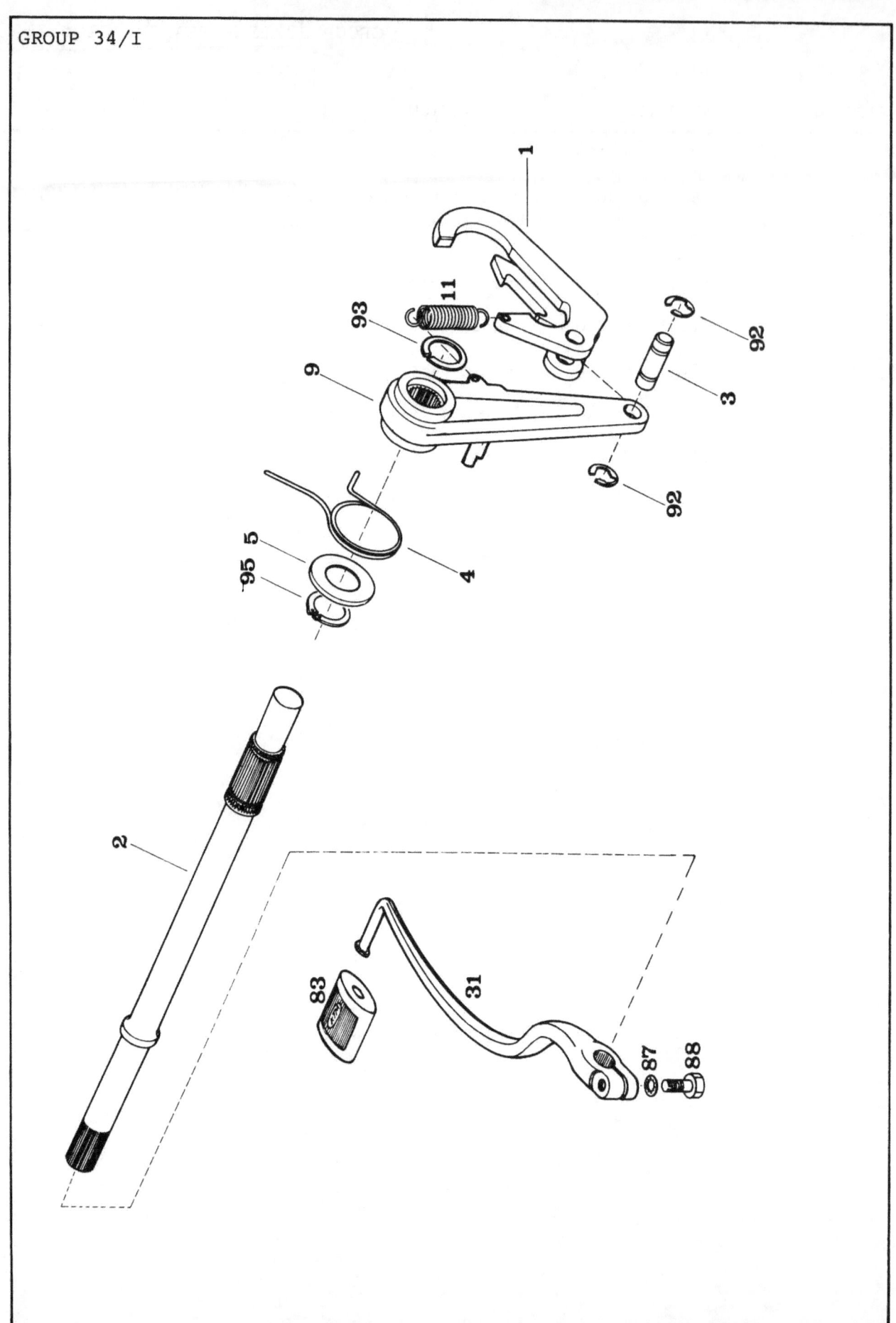

62

GROUP 34/I - SHIFTING MECHANISM I

PICTURE	PART NO.	DESCRIPTION	125	175	250	400
1	52.34.001.400	Shifting quadrant	1	1	1	1
2	52.34.002.500	Shifting shaft	1	1	1	1
3	51.34.003.300	Pin	1	1	1	1
4	51.34.004.100	Returning spring	1	1	1	1
5	51.34.005.300	Washer for spring	1	1	1	1
9	51.34.009.500	Shift lever internal	1	1	1	1
11	51.34.011.000	Shift lever spring	1	1	1	1
31	51.34.031.400	Shift lever with part 83 & screw	1	1	1	1
83	32.03.083.000	Rubber, shift lever	1	1	1	1
87	0127 060000	Lock washer A 6 DIN 127	1	1	1	1
88	0931 060253	Hexagon head screw M 6x25	1	1	1	1
92	0799 070000	Retaining clip 7 DIN -799	1	1	1	1
93	52.34.093.000	Circlip	1	1	1	1
95	0471 171500	Circlip	2	2	2	2

GROUP 34/II

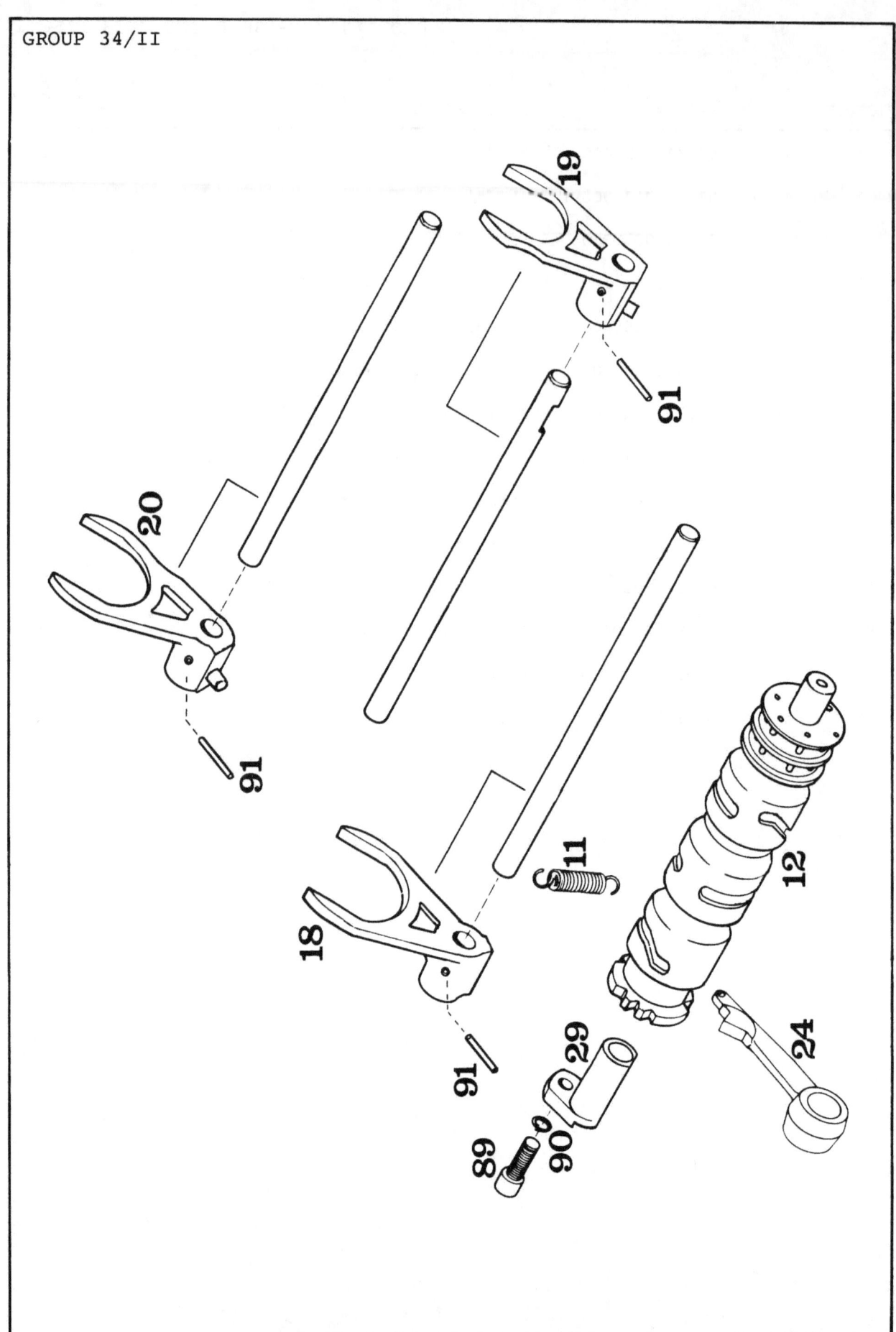

GROUP 34/II - SHIFTING MECHANISM II

PICTURE	PART NO.	DESCRIPTION	125	175	250	400
11	51.34.011.000	Shift lever spring	1	1	1	1
12	54.34.012.206	Shifting drum for 6 speed cpl. GS	1	1	1	1
-	54.34.012.205	Shifting drum for 5 speed cpl. MC	1	1	1	1
18	54.34.018.044	*Assemby-Shifting rod with shifting fork 1st/3rd gear	1	1	1	1
19	54.34.019.044	*Assembly-Shifting rod with shifting fork 2nd /4th gear	1	1	1	1
20	54.34.020.044	*Assembly-Shifting rod with shifting fork 5th/6th gear	1	1	1	1
24	51.34.024.200	Locating lever	1	1	-	-
-	55.34.024.200	Locating lever	-	-	1	1
29	51.34.029.500	Bushing for shifting drum	1	1	1	1
89	0912 060163	Allen head screw M 6x16 DIN 912	1	1	1	1
90	0137 060000	Spring washer B 6 DIN 137	1	1	1	1
91	0481 030180	Roll on pin 3x18	3	3	3	3

* Completely assembled

VELOCEPRESS MANUALS – MOTORCYCLE BY MAKE

AJS 1932-1948 SINGLES & TWINS 250cc THRU 1000cc (BOOK OF)
AJS 1945-1956 SINGLES RIGID & SPRTING FACTORY WSM & PARTS
AJS 1945-1960 SINGLES MODELS 16 & 18 350cc & 500cc (BOOK OF)
AJS 1948-1956 TWINS MODELS 20 & 30 FACTORY WSM & PARTS
AJS 1955-1965 SINGLES MODELS 16 & 18 350cc & 500cc (BOOK OF)
AJS 1957-1966 SINGLES & TWINS (ALL) FACTORY WSM
AJS 1959-1969 G80CS G85CS & P11 OFF ROAD FACTORY WSM
AJS 1968-1974 STORMER FACTORY WSM & PARTS LIST
ARIEL UP TO 1932 (BOOK OF)
ARIEL 1932-1939 PREWAR MODELS (BOOK OF)
ARIEL 1933-1951 (WORKSHOP MANUAL)
ARIEL 1939-1960 4 STROKE SINGLES (BOOK OF)
ARIEL 1958-1964 LEADER & ARROW FACTORY WSM & PARTS LIST
ARIEL 1958-1964 LEADER & ARROW (BOOK OF)
BMW R26 R27 (1956-1967) FACTORY WORKSHOP MANUAL
BMW R50 R50S R60 R69S (1955-1969) FACTORY WORKSHOP MANUAL
BMW R50/5 R60/5 R75/5 (1969-1973) FACTORY WORKSHOP MANUAL
BRIDGESTONE 90 SERIES FACTORY WSM & PARTS CATALOGUE
BRIDGESTONE 175 SERIES FACTORY WSM & PARTS CATALOGUE
BRIDGESTONE 350 SERIES FACTORY WSM & PARTS CATALOGUES
BSA SERVICE SHEETS MASTER CATALOGUE ALL MODELS 1945-1967
BSA BANTAM D1 TO D7 1948-1966 FACTORY SERVICE SHEETS MANUAL
BSA BANTAM ALL MODELS FROM 1948 ONWARDS (BOOK OF)
BSA BANTAM D14 FACTORY SERVICE MANUAL
BSA DANDY FACTORY WORKSHOP MANUAL (COMPILATION)
BSA SINGLES & V-TWINS UP TO 1926 inc. 1927 SUPPLEMENT (BOOK OF)
BSA SINGLES & V-TWINS UP TO 1930 (BOOK OF)
BSA SINGLES & V-TWINS UP TO 1935 (BOOK OF)
BSA SINGLES & V-TWINS 1936-1939 (BOOK OF)
BSA C10, C11 & C12 1945-1958 FACTORY SERVICE SHEETS MANUAL
BSA OHV & SV SINGLES 250-600cc 1945-1959 (BOOK OF)
BSA C15 & B40 1958-1967 FACTORY SERVICE SHEETS MANUAL
BSA OHV & SV SINGLES 250cc (ONLY) 1954-1970 (BOOK OF)
BSA B31, B32, B33 & B34 1945-60 FACTORY SERVICE SHEETS MANUAL
BSA OHV SINGLES 350 & 500cc 1955-1967 (BOOK OF)
BSA M20, M21 & M33 1945-1963 FACTORY SERVICE SHEETS MANUAL
BSA TWINS A7 & A10 1948-1962 FACTORY SERVICE SHEETS MANUAL
BSA TWINS A7 & A10 1948-1962 (BOOK OF)
BSA TWINS A50 & A65 1962-1965 FACTORY WORKSHOP MANUAL
BSA TWINS A50 & A65 1962-1969 (SECOND BOOK OF)
BULTACO 125cc to 37cc SINGLES 1968-1979 WORKSHOP MANUAL
CZ 125cc to 380cc SINGLES 1967-1974 WORKSHOP MANUAL
DOUGLAS 1929-1939 PREWAR ALL MODELS (BOOK OF)
DOUGLAS 1948-1957 POSTWAR ALL MODELS FACTORY SHOP MANUAL
DUCATI 160cc, 250cc & 350cc OHC MODELS FACTORY SHOP MANUAL
HODAKA 90cc,100cc & 125cc SINGLES 1964-1978 WORKSHOP MANUAL
HONDA 50cc ALL MODELS UP TO 1970 INC MONKEY & TRAIL (BOOK OF)
HONDA 90cc ALL MODELS UP TO 1966 (BOOK OF)
HONDA TWINS & SINGLES 50cc THRU 305cc 1960-1966 (BOOK OF)
HONDA TWINS ALL MODELS 125cc THRU 450cc UP TO 1968 (BOOK OF)
HONDA C100 50cc SUPER CUB O.H.C. 1959-1962 FACTORY WSM
HONDA C110 50cc SPORT CUB O.H.C. 1960-1962 FACTORY WSM
HONDA 50-65-70-90cc O.H.C. SINGLES 1959-1983 WSM
HONDA 100-125cc SINGLES CB/CD/CL/SL/TL 1970-1984 FACTORY WSM
HONDA 125-150cc TWINS C/CS/CB/CA 1959-1966 FACTORY WSM
HONDA 125-160-175-200cc TWINS 1965-1978 WORKSHOP MANUAL
HONDA 250-305cc TWINS C/CS/CB 1961-1968 FACTORY WSM
HOHDA 250-350cc TWINS CB/CL/SL 1968-1973 FACTORY WSM
HONDA 250-360cc TWINS CB/CL/CJ 1974-1977 FACTORY WSM
HONDA 350F & 400F 4-CYLINDER 1972-1977 FACTORY WSM
HONDA 450cc TWINS CB/CL 1965-1974 K0 TO K7 WORKSHOP MANUAL
HONDA 500cc & 550cc 4-CYL 1971-1978 FACTORY WORKSHOP MANUAL
HONDA 750cc SHOC 4-CYL 1969-1978 K0~K8 WORKSHOP MANUAL
HUSQVARNA 125cc to 450cc SINGLES 1965-1975 WORKSHOP MANUAL
INDIAN PONYBIKE, BOY RACER & PAPOOSE ILL PARTS LIST & SALES LIT

J.A.P. ENGINES 1927-1952 & MOTORCYCLES 1934-1952 (BOOK OF)
MAICO 250cc to 501cc 1968-1978 WORKSHOP MANUAL
MATCHLESS 1931-1939 ALL MODELS 250cc THRU 990cc (BOOK OF)
MATCHLESS 1945-1956 RIGID & SPRING FACTORY WSM & PARTS
MATCHLESS 1945-1956 SINGLES G3 & G80 350cc & 500cc (BOOK OF)
MATCHLESS 1948-1956 TWINS G9 & G11 FACTORY WSM & PARTS
MATCHLESS 1955-1966 SINGLES G3 & G80 350cc & 500cc (BOOK OF)
MATCHLESS 1957-1966 SINGLES & TWINS (ALL) FACTORY WSM
MONTESA 1962-1978 125cc to 360cc ALL MODELS WORKSHOP MANUAL
NEW IMPERIAL ALL SV & OHV FROM 1935 ONWARDS (BOOK OF)
NORTON 1932-1939 PREWAR MODELS (BOOK OF)
NORTON 1932-1947 (BOOK OF)
NORTON 1938-1956 (BOOK OF)
NORTON 1945-1963 MODELS 16H, Big4, ES2, 19 & 50 WSM'S & PARTS
NORTON 1955-1963 MODELS 19, 50 & ES2 (BOOK OF)
NORTON 1948-1970 DOMINATOR TWINS FACTORY WSM'S & PARTS
NORTON 1955-1965 DOMINATOR TWINS (BOOK OF)
NORTON 1960-1970 TWIN CYLINDER FACTORY WORKSHOP MANUAL
NORTON 1970-1975 COMMANDO 850 & 750cc FACTORY WSM
NORTON 1975-1978 MK 3 COMMANDO 850 cc FACTORY WSM
PANTHER 1932-1958 LIGHTWEIGHT MODELS 250 & 350cc (BOOK OF)
PANTHER 1938-1966 HEAVYWEIGHT MODELS 600 & 650cc (BOOK OF)
PENTON-KTM-SACHS 1968-1975 100cc & 125cc WORKSHOP MANUAL
PENTON-KTM 1972-1975 175cc, 250cc & 400cc WSM & PARTS MANUALS
PENTON-KTM 1972-1979 125cc to 400cc ENGINE WSM & PARTS MANUAL
RALEIGH MOTORCYCLES 1919-1933 (BOOK OF)
ROYAL ENFIELD 1934-1946 SINGLES & V TWINS (BOOK OF)
ROYAL ENFIELD 1937-1953 SINGLES & V TWINS (BOOK OF)
ROYAL ENFIELD 1946-1962 SINGLES (BOOK OF)
ROYAL ENFIELD 1948-1962 350cc & 500cc PRE-UNIT BULLET WSM
ROYAL ENFIELD 1948-1963 SINGLES FACTORY WORKSHOP MANUAL
ROYAL ENFIELD 1952-1963 700cc TWINS FACTORY WORKSHOP MANUAL
ROYAL ENFIELD 1956-1966 250cc CRUSADER & 350cc NEW BULLET WSM
ROYAL ENFIELD 1958-1966 250cc & 350cc SINGLES (SECOND BOOK OF)
ROYAL ENFIELD 1962-1970 INTERCEPTOR WSM'S & PARTS (Compilation)
RUDGE 1933-1939 (BOOK OF)
SACHS 1968-1975 100cc & 125cc ENGINES WSM & M/CYCLE PARTS LIST
SUNBEAM 1928-1939 (BOOK OF)
SUNBEAM 1946-1957 S7 & S8 (BOOK OF)
SUZUKI 50cc & 80cc UP TO 1966 (BOOK OF)
SUZUKI T10 1963-1967 FACTORY WORKSHOP MANUAL
SUZUKI T20 & T200 1965-1969 FACTORY WORKSHOP MANUAL
SUZUKI TWINS 1962 ONWARDS 125-500cc WORKSHOP MANUAL
TRIUMPH 1935-1949 SINGLES & TWINS (BOOK OF)
TRIUMPH 1937-1961 SINGLES SV & OHV 250cc-600cc + TERRIER & CUB
TRIUMPH 1945-1955 PRE-UNIT 350cc, 500cc & 650cc TWINS WSM No.11
TRIUMPH 1945-1959 TWINS (BOOK OF)
TRIUMPH 1956-1969 TWINS (BOOK OF)
TRIUMPH 1956-1962 PRE-UNIT 500cc & 650cc TWINS WSM No.17
TRIUMPH 1957-1963 UNIT CONSTRUCTION 350-500cc WSM No.4
TRIUMPH 1963-1974 UNIT CONSTRUCTION 350-500cc FACTORY WSM
TRIUMPH 1963-1970 UNIT CONSTRUCTION 650cc FACTORY WSM
TRIUMPH 1968-1974 TRIDENT T150 & T150V FACTORY WSM
TRIUMPH 1971-1973 650cc OIL-IN-FRAME FACTORY WSM
TRIUMPH 1973-1978 750cc BONNEVILLE & TIGER FACTORY WSM
TRIUMPH 1979-1983 T140, TR7 & TR65 FACTORY WSM
VELOCETTE 1925-1970 ALL SINGLES & TWINS (BOOK OF)
VELOCETTE 1933-1952 MOV-MAC-MSS RIGID FRAME FACTORY WSM
VELOCETTE 1953-1960 MAC SPRING FRAME WSM & ILL PARTS LIST
VELOCETTE 1954-1971 MSS-VENOM-THRUXTON-VIPER FACTORY WSM
VILLIERS ENGINE UP TO 1959 INC. 3 WHEELERS (BOOK OF)
VILLIERS ENGINE UP TO 1969 (BOOK OF)
VINCENT 1935-1955 (WORKSHOP MANUAL)
YAMAHA 1961-1967 YA5 & YA6 (WORKSHOP MANUAL & ILL PARTS LIST)
YAMAHA 1968-1971 DT1 & MX SERIES Inc. GYT WORKSHOP MANUAL
YAMAHA 1971-1972 JT1& JT2 (WORKSHOP MANUAL & ILL PARTS LIST)

VELOCEPRESS MANUALS – SCOOTERS BY MAKE

BSA SUNBEAM SCOOTER WORKSHOP MANUAL 1959-1965
BSA SUNBEAM SCOOTER 1959-1965 (BOOK OF)
LAMBRETTA 1947-1957 ALL 125 & 150cc MODELS (BOOK OF)
LAMBRETTA 1957-1970 LI & TV MODELS (SECOND BOOK OF)
NSU PRIMA 1956-1964 ALL MODELS (BOOK OF)
TRIUMPH TIGRESS SCOOTER WORKSHOP MANUAL 1959-1965
TRIUMPH TIGRESS SCOOTER (BOOK OF)
VESPA 1951-1961 (BOOK OF)
VESPA 1955-1963 125 & 150cc & GS MODELS (SECOND BOOK OF)
VESPA 1955-1968 GS & SS (BOOK OF)
VESPA 1963-1972 90, 125 & 150cc (THIRD BOOK OF)

VELOCEPRESS MANUALS – MOPEDS & MOTORIZED BICYCLES

CYCLEMOTOR (BOOK OF)
NSU QUICKLY 1953-1963 ALL MODELS (BOOK OF)
PUCH MAXI N & S MAINTENANCE & REPAIR (3 MANUAL COMPILATION)
RALEIGH MOPEDS 1960-1969 (BOOK OF)

VELOCEPRESS MANUALS - THREE WHEELER'S

BOND MINICAR THREE WHEELER 1948-1967 (BOOK OF)
BMW ISETTA FACTORY WORKSHOP MANUAL
BSA THREE WHEELER (BOOK OF)
RELIANT REGAL THREE WHEELER 1952-1973 (BOOK OF)
VINTAGE MORGAN THREE WHEELER (BOOK OF)

VELOCEPRESS TECHNICAL BOOKS – MOTORCYCLE

1930'S BRITISH MOTORCYCLE CARBS & ELEC COMPONENTS (BOOK OF)
1930'S BRITISH MOTORCYCLE ENGINES (OVERHAUL & MAINTENANCE)
1930'S BRITISH MOTORCYCLE GEARBOXES & CLUTCHES (BOOK OF)
CATALOG OF BRITISH MOTORCYCLES (1951 MODELS)
LUCAS ELECTRONICS BRITISH M/CYCLES REPAIR & PARTS (1950-1977)
MOTORCYCLE ENGINEERING (P.E. Irving)
MOTORCYCLE ROAD TESTS 1949-1953 (Motor Cycle Magazine UK)
SPEED AND HOW TO OBTAIN IT (Motor Cycle Magazine UK)
TUNING FOR SPEED (P.E. Irving)
WIPAC (COMBO) MANUAL NUMBER 3 + M/CYCLE & SCOOTER MANUAL

www.ingramcontent.com/pod-product-compliance
Lightning Source LLC
Chambersburg PA
CBHW080747300426
44114CB00019B/2669